ARKANSAS MEN
AT WAR

By

JAMES GUY TUCKER, JR.

Library of Congress Catalog Card Number: 68-29339

Tucker, James Guy Jr.
Arkansas Men at War
Little Rock, Ark.   The Pioneer Press
May 1, 1968

                                        4-12-68

INTRODUCTION

In the following pages Jim Guy Tucker ably presents a factual account of the war in Vietnam as it affects men from our home state of Arkansas.

This book does not portray a romantic war with massed ranks of brilliantly clad soldiers and color guards led by mounted officers advancing to meet an enemy similarly outfitted, equipped and led. Nor is it about a war fought by religious fanatics with the emblem of the cross emblazoned on their armor.

This war offers no vestige of the pomp and pageantry that marked the legendary efforts of the 3rd Arkansas at Gettysburg. Conversely there is none of the fanatical excesses that marked the retaking of Jerusalem by the European Crusaders.

There are few epic encounters on a grandiose scale in this war. It is marked by highly personalized encounters between men using sophisticated and highly deadly weapons.

But no amount of refinement in the engines of war can remove the brutality and suffering of all—combatants and noncombatants—who come in contact with this melancholy endeavor.

Death is just as sudden and final to the soldier from Helena whose jeep strikes an enemy mine in Vietnam as it was to his great grandfather who rode into cannon fire at Shiloh. Mr. Tucker has made this graphically clear in his reporting. I am hopeful that this account of the war—stripped of all the false glamour and glory of novel and screenplay—will help to create a better understanding of the men we send to fight our wars, and the motivation of those of us who seek to find a solution that will result in a cessation of this armed conflict which is daily claiming the lives of our friends, our neighbors, our fellow Arkansans and our fellow Americans.

Until this solution is found and accepted by those in a position to halt this war we must continue to support—as we have consistently supported in the past—every measure that is necessary for the strength, safety, and comfort of our men in the field.

J. W. FULBRIGHT

DECEMBER 25, 1967

PREFACE

Any comment on the war in Vietnam calls forth speculation on the political position of the author. My own views of the war do not coincide with the doctrinaire stiffness of either the "hawks" or the "doves." But my political, military, or moral opinions are unimportant.

My sole purpose in collecting these stories is to provide a clearer view of the daily life of Arkansas men at war. For those who never will live in the agony, and the boredom, of a war zone, I hope this book will provide insight through the words and experiences of our Arkansas neighbors, relatives, and friends.

I express my sincere appreciation to Charles Murphy of the National Broadcasting Company, and Ken Danforth of TIME for always providing a place to stay in Saigon.

My good friends Jim McDougal, Jack Files, Roger Armbrust, and Lawrence Harper were great help in encouraging this undertaking and seeing it through to the end.

For their cooperation in financing my reporting, thanks to:

Arkansas Democrat; Batesville Daily Guard and Record; Conway Log Cabin Democrat; Crossett News Observer; Harrison Daily News; Jonesboro Evening Sun; Northwest Arkansas Times; Russellville Courier Democrat; Searcy Daily Citizen; The Southwest American; West Memphis Evening Times; Fayetteville, Winter, 1967

1965

July 14, 1965

Looking at the truckloads full of United States soldiers arriving at the Bien Hoa airbase yesterday afternoon, Lt. Col. Lloyd "Scooter" Burke of Stuttgart, winner of the Congressional Medal of Honor in Korea, said, "We're here to kill VC, we are going to patrol, search them out, and when we find them, we're going to kill them."

Most of the soldiers in Burke's 2nd Battalion 16th Infantry have never seen combat. Forty to sixty percent of them are draftees. Their organization, though a part of the highly spirited, Big Red First Division, is not a volunteer outfit. The young men who are settling into their defensive positions at the Bien Hoa airbase are typical American "citizen soldiers." They have a two year tour of duty in the Army, and then return to their civilian status . . . the era when Vietnam was a professional soldier's war is now over. American casualties will shortly be announced not one or two at a time . . . but quite likely in the same numbers that Vietnamese casualties have been announced for so long.

The question arises as to the reaction of the American people when they suddenly do realize that Vietnam is a place where a great many Americans are likely to die. Lt. Col. Burke points out, quite correctly, that the men arriving here from the

1

states are fully aware that they are indeed soldiers, and that they may be killed here. But, what will happen as the American people watch the casualty figures among American troops start to build?

The American citizenry has not been prepared to accept reports of heavy American casualties. As a matter of fact, they are still tremendously upset when they hear of only four or five Americans being killed in a battle. Most Americans are presently blithely unaware of the fact that "those little brown men" way over in Vietnam can actually inflict any serious damage to the mighty American monolith. In short, most Americans just haven't realized there is a real war here.

America's dangerous ignorance of the true situation in Vietnam is due to several causes. First, the Americans don't like to think about war . . . they listen only lightly to the news from here, and forget quickly. Second, press reports have seldom emphasized the massive death toll suffered by the Vietnamese in this war, and as a result most Americans think the death toll here is pretty low. They fail to translate actual Vietnamese deaths to potential American deaths.

The American soldier is one of the world's best fighting men. But he is certainly not invulnerable. The newly arrived Americans will soon realize what this name "Vietcong" really means. He may have been told that the VC are tough, resourceful, ruthless fighters. But he has been told that he is better. There is no doubt in my mind that American soldiers can defeat the Vietcong. But the fact remains, that no matter how fierce the fighter, when an American heliborne battalion is dropped into a clearing surrounded by Vietcong machineguns and mortars, it will be slaughtered just as quickly as a Vietnamese battalion.

It is a chance that soldiers know they must take. I'm not sure the American citizenry knows, or wants to admit, that their boys are now taking that chance.

Shortly before the First Division started landing at Bien Hoa yesterday the VC mortared a village only 2,000 meters away from the landing zone. Small arms fire continued for fifteen minutes. Artillery was firing in the distance as the planes approached, but it was unfortunately quiet when the troops stepped off their plane.

Those young men were serious and professional as they made their camp last night . . . but it's a shame they missed the mortaring because they are going to learn very quickly the facts of this war . . . and someone needs to start reminding the American people, as much as they do hate to be reminded, what war is all about.

2

1967

This is the story of three Arkansas boys and how they passed the time on July 4, 1967, this third year of our war. They spent this Fourth of July hiding from sniper fire and waiting to move a hundred yards forward to recover the bodies of seventy Marine friends who had been killed two days before.

The DMZ dividing North and South Vietnam is a flat, barren area, filled only with scrub brush, hedgerows, shell craters, and bodies. On July 2, a company of the Third Battalion, Ninth Marines ran into, or were ambushed by, a strong North Vietnamese force that had crossed the Ben Hai River and was roaming south towards the Marine outpost of Con Thien. Before the battle was over, at least seventy Marines were dead and 170 wounded. The fighting continued sporadically for three days as the Marines pushed slowly forward to recover their dead.

James Larry Howard, 21, son of Mr. and Mrs. Homer Howard of Bright (Miller County), Floyd E. Bradley, 19, son of Mrs. Edith Bradley and the late Mr. Bradley of Shirley (Van Buren County), and Billy E. Davis, 18, son of Mr. and Mrs. Elmer C. Shepard of Pine Bluff, were at the forefront of this action. A walk to their position was an education in the desolation of war.

In the helicopter landing zone, half-naked Marine stretcher bearers moved like wraiths through a dreamlike haze of choking

3

red dust. Nerves straining almost as visibly as their tendons, they lifted their torn comrades onto the rescue ships, then stumbled dizzily back to the wounded waiting on chairs of splintered logs and crushed metal. Also waiting, dust covered and still, were the remains of what had once been friends, husbands, brothers—living boys a few hours before. One dead Marine had been placed under a poncho to keep the flies away and to keep his staring eyes from the sight of his former companions who still lived. He was quite young and his wounds hardly visible. His trousers fluttered in the occasional breeze that blows along that barren stretch . . . next to him lay the possessions he carried with him on his last day. Most were tools of war; a torn helmet, flak jacket; broken rifle. Also there was a photo and a letter, the address blurred by his sweat.

Further forward, Marines with haunted eyes admonished, "Don't. Don't go up there. Snipers!" The trail narrows and empties. A gutted tank, shell casings, a torn shirt, empty boxes and C ration cans—part of the litter of war—lay scattered along the trail. Stumbling to the rear came the walking wounded, some with heads, legs, hands bandaged and lips compressed with pain. Others had no visible wounds. These were concussion victims, gasping, or shaking their heads to clear some invisible fog, they dragged themselves through the dust absolutely silent, oblivious to any sniper fire. No one else was seen except the silent sentries, the friendly dead, stretched by the side of the path.

Across some torn strands of barbed wire, in a twenty foot deep bomb crater stood Larry Howard. Another Marine was standing there with ten canteens full of water he had just brought back from the five gallon water cans on the tanks further up. Larry had come to the 'line' at dawn this morning carrying his usual load of 3.5 millimeter rockets. Each round weighs nine pounds . . . Larry carried three, plus his pack, his rifle, three canteens, a 12 pound flak jacket, steel helmet— a total of nearly 75 pounds. Shell craters were large and small, some filled yet with the black strench of gunpowder, or the ugly grey of shrapnel, others clean and smooth, their rawness somewhat disguised by the dust sliding and blowing into the wounded earth.

Larry used to help make the things that had made those holes when he worked on the assembly line at the Red River Army Depot. Now he knows how much a man should fear them. "The artillery and mortars are the most frightening," he says. "You can hear them coming but you never know whether it will hit you or not.

You do know it will hurt if it does," he says softly. "The

thought of it is the worst." For Larry, it's hard to think of death having anything but the deep bass roar of an exploding mortar shell.

His helmet has his wife's name, Brenda, printed in indelible ink across the camouflage covering. His wife is the former Brenda Dishaw daughter of Mr. and Mrs. C. W. Griffin of Texarkana, Ark., and Atlanta, Tex.

"When I get home I just want to find some place quiet and peaceful. I've seen more in the last month than in my whole life. Some of these guys here really don't mind dying for their country. They do things I never believed anyone could do."

Larry looked over the edge of his hole to where the planes were bombing. "Oh yeah, say 'hi' to Clive Griffin, for me. He's a good buddy." He pointed forward to a line of six tanks. "Bradley is up there."

Before Floyd Bradley moved to Van Buren County, and before he came to Vietnam, he used to live in Little Rock. He went to school at Fuller and likes to fish. "If I was back home today I'd be eating watermelon and fishing on the White River. A river! Boy one of those would look good right now. I'm so thirsty! We can't get enough water up here!"

Floyd's helmet is also decorated. Across the front is emblazoned the word 'Hillbilly'. On the right side is written, "The South Shall Rise Again."

He kept ducking his head as the jets screamed down and then upward overhead, spitting out their seedlike bombs that blossomed into any one of a half dozen "deadly flowers," spreading their petals of fiery savage death.

Death came in six colors three hundreds yards out where the bombs were landing. The napalm has a black lace mantle with deep orange center; as it struck the ground it sent a long white pistel soaring upward before its blossom opened. The five-hundred pounders raised a cloud of red brown; the thousand pounders mushroomed in a graceful, spreading web of black speckled with darker fragments of earth and shrapnel.

"We came out to pick up the bodies," said Bradley. "So far we've only been able to get three. But when the wind is right you can tell there's a lot more out there."

"Hey, there's another guy from Arkansas in Kilo Company right up there by the bombs, Davis is his name; he's from Pine Bluff, I think.

Billy E. Davis, ("Bill is what they call me") graduated from Sheridan High School in 1966. As he came dodging toward his foxhole it was apparent that he considered the explosions only a few hundred yards away, much, much too close. "Boy, those bodies we brought out last night were in pretty bad condition," he said. "By the time those planes get through with that area they're really going to be torn up. Bill is an eighteen-year-old Marine Lance Corporal and machine gunner. He's not as scared now as he was before, he says. "You get used to it, I guess."

"I was really jumpy the first night I was on the line. My buddy was asleep in his poncho on some sandbags next to our foxhole. About two in the morning, when it was real dark, he rolled over in his sleep and fell on me. Gee! I thought it was the Vietcong that had jumped on me and I started hitting him and yelling. It was funny," he said with a nervous chuckle.

A jet seemed to brush the trees as it pulled out of its dive; shrapnel pelted down around Bill. His company commander threw out a green smoke grenade to mark his men's position for the pilots.

Across from Bill lay a stack of folded blue green 'body bags'. One rubber container lay sprawled, its zippered mouth open waiting for its cargo, waiting for the Friendly Dead.

"Charlie ain't nobody's fool!" That's how Sgt. Gregory Gray, late of Batesville, presently making him home with the U.S. Army in Di An, Vietnam looks at his enemy.

"Charlie is a good fighter," says Gray, and Gray knows what he's talking about. For the last three months he has been in action almost continuously. Today he sits in a Vietnamese turnip patch guarding the western flank of his battalion which is searching the village of Hoa Nhut. His eyes scan the jungle on the other side of two Buddhist grave markers.

"I've been spending most of my time on 'search and destroy' operations; the choppers carry us into an area, we climb off, then we start walking."

The kind of walking Gray speaks of means temperatures of 100 degrees, literally millions of malaria-carrying mosquitoes, and the constant agony of knowing every step you take may be your last. A walk in a Vietnamese jungle means trying to see every branch of every tree to make sure it does not hide a sniper; it means shivering as you touch each bush—because it may be booby trapped; it means walking over tunnel systems 30 feet underground that conceal a whole company of Vietcong; and finally it means a separate prayer for each footstep. Everytime Gregory Gray places his foot in the moss and mud and rotting wood of the jungle floor he must expect a mine to envelope him and tear him apart with its explosion.

Last month on Operation Manhattan in the Ong Gong jungle, Sgt. Gray captured two Vietcong. He was directing his squad down a stream bed with two men searching the bushes on either side. The foliage was far too thick to see more than a few feet in any direction. Then came the sudden confrontation of one of Gray's men with the VC.

"I heard my man yell 'Halt!' " said Gray. "When I ran

7

over it turned out this VC had just walked right into him. As I turned back around, another Charlie came out of the bushes. He didn't know we were there either. So we caught them both."

Gray says he didn't have time to be scared; it just happened too fast— very much like the heat and speed of an early fall football game at Batesville High School where Greg used to play defensive tackle. He did not finish high school. But in the future he'll be able to cite his education as "Vietnam, Class of '67."

What else does he run into in the jungle? "The other day we were in a place called the Heartshaped Jungle," says Gregory. "We knocked down one of those 'anthills' and got about seven weapons.

"The 'anthills' average about three, four, maybe five feet. The VC can hide weapons or make headquarters out of them."

Shortly after midnight today Sgt. Gray and men like him surrounded Hoa Nhut, hoping to trap inside any Vietcong who were in the Village.

Gray's job was to keep those Vietcong trapped in the village and not let them slip through the "seal" the Americans had set up around the town. Escaping certainly would have been difficult for there were about two dozen tanks surrounding the village with over five hundred soldiers supporting them.

Today Sgt. Gray, dressed in sweat-soaked jungle fatigues, will be in his foxhole in this soft green field for 12 hours. Then he will walk back out, across the small blue flowers in this field, through a small stream, climb onto a tank and then ride back to a hot tent and a cold beer . . . until the next time he is ordered back into the jungle, for another day's routine work.

He says "hello" to his mother, Mrs. Harry Paul, an old buddy, Bobby Brown, and especially, to "Susie."

Five more Arkansans were found at Hoa Nhut; two were unable to be contacted. They were Sp4 Willie Johnson of McCrory (Woodruff County) and PFC Ronald Staggs of Harrison.

Di An Vietnam, June 16, 1967

"We've got a big job to do over here. It's a lot of fun to try."

That is the simple explanation that introduces a reporter to Capt. Don Hatfield of Fort Smith, a tall, handsome, twenty-five year old soldier who is information officer for the 2nd Brigade, First Division. Today he is working in the village of Hoa Nhut on a "search and seal" mission.

"I work with American and Vietnamese press in publicizing 'revolutionary development'," explains Hatfield. "Revolutionary development is the term that we're using now for what the French called "pacification." We try to get the Vietnamese people to realize that the South Vietnamese government is working for them. We co-operate with government forces in trying to accomplish this mission."

But Hatfield knows that it isn't all fun. His predecessor was seriously injured by a mine explosion while moving through an operation only two miles from here last month. His job calls for all the hardships of fighting a war with the added inconvenience of trying to explain the war to often dissatisfied and ill-tempered members of the press.

"We're working in the toughest area of Vietnam," says Don. "It has a history of underworld organization that predates the Vietcong by almost 100 years.

"It's one of the most heavily populated areas in the country, roughly half a million. We figure if we can crack this nut we can pretty much take care of the whole country."

Don sincerely believes the Army's task of "winning the hearts and minds of the people" is succeeding. "We have definitely made a lot of progress. I also know that we have a long way to go. I think we can accomplish this job here, given enough time and given enough support. But it will take a long time."

The time seemed short in Hoa Nhut. Though the predominate attitude of the people had been sullen, resentful and frightened when the troops first arrived in the village at dawn, a few hours later the population was actually almost all smiles.

Before the smiles, Hatfield pointed out three young men lying face down at the edge of the road. These men were suspected of an attempted breach of the "seal" of U.S. troops around the village. They were suspected of being Vietcong. They and all others in the village who do not have proper identification, or who have been reported to have been engaged in activity with the Vietcong, are interrogated at length by American intelligence officers working with Vietnamese interpreters.

Capt. Hatfield explained that the vast majority of these people are released; but a few are sent on to Saigon for further questioning and investigation.

The questions asked the suspects vary: "Who is the local Vietcong leader? How often do the Vietcong collect taxes here? When was the last time a group of guerrillas moved through this village? Have you ever planted any mines for the Vietcong? Sold them rice? Carried rice for them?"

Captain Hatfield, who graduated in 1963 from Arkansas Tech in Russellville, has been in Vietnam a little over a month. As he gently negotiated his jeep around the deep pits in the road, he occasionally adjusted the plastic bottle of bug repellant that he keeps in the band around his camouflaged helmet, and he spoke of home and future plans.

9

Don's wife, Katherine, is presently in Fayetteville working on a degree in art at the University of Arkansas. She is, he says, deeply missed. Capt. Hatfield is the son of Mr. and Mrs. H. D. Hatfield of Fort Smith. His sister, Mrs. Bill Kiehl, is living in Russellville.

Di An Vietnam, June 16, 1967

As Sgt. Elmer Taylor of Pochahontas, goes up Route 13 into Hoa Nhut, it is about six o'clock in the morning; his jeep carries him through Lambrettas, Vespas, Hondas, and other small motor bikes traveling the dirt road on their way to market or work. The sides of all the roads are strung with great coils of rusty barbed wide, decorated like some psychedelic christmas tree with empty tin cans that jangle and warn the guard houses along the road of any attempted breach of the barrier.

The sun has a greenish tone so early in the morning as it reflects on the scum and the tender grass along the rice paddy dikes. Buddhist shrines cast their colorful roofs high over the tops of the mud-brown palm and straw huts of the villages.

Occasionally Sgt. Taylor passes a high concrete wall topped with sharp, jagged pieces of green and ochre colored glass designed to guard . . . whoever or whatever inside is in need of being guarded.

In the town of Phu Loi, just outside of Hoa Nhut, his jeep throws clouds of dust across the fronts of a long line of bars whose customers are not Vietnamese. The names of the bars: Olympia, Sweet Suzie, China Doll, Sexy, Shootin' Star, GiGi, Virginia, Jacqueline.

Then Taylor rolls past ox-drawn carts with wooden wheels higher than the oxen themselves. The oxen turn their heads to watch Taylor come by, and then continue to stare at the convoy that follows.

The people of the village have seen this same scene many times before. So some stand, hand on hip, or arms clasped behind their back, and watch the troops move by. Others stay inside the huts, huts filled with the wet, warm smell of breakfast and the pungency of the smoldering "Joss" sticks. ("Joss" means "Good luck" or "Good fortune".)

Yet others are busy with the normal tasks of village life; drawing water from the well, feeding the pigs and chickens, tending the water wheel at the village creek, waiting for a bus to Saigon. All are dressed in the village "uniform" of loose black or white pajamas and sandals. In the village everything and everybody is damp with humidity or sweat.

10

A few of the newly arrived Americans wave at the children and villagers along the roadside. Occasionally they get a wave or smile in reply; but for the most part they receive only a dull, vacant stare from the people. The Americans who have been here for some time don't bother to wave; they stare fixedly ahead through the dust of the convoy.

As Sgt. Taylor turns into the village where he is working today several oxen calves are playing in a Buddist grave yard. Those baby bovines seem about the only living thing here that is unconcerned and unresentful.

Taylor's job is with "the other war" in Vietnam: winning the people. Today he is directing a "pacification" operation. This is the fifth time such an operation has been carried out in this village, and Sgt. Taylor feels the program is "working".

Although official terminology for this performance is "seal and search", the Americans call it "a county fair", because after the military has searched the village, medical teams hold sick call, bands play, and Vietnamese clowns and singers perform.

A soft-spoken and warm man, Taylor enjoys talking about the "fair." "We do anything we can to get a big crowd and try to make a few friends," he says. "Most places we have good response; many people come.

"We pass out goodies to the kids: candy, toys. Some of the little fellas are afraid of the doctors, but they're happy when they leave. They're mostly bolder than state-side children. They'll come up and talk to you, or try to, much more than an American child."

"I volunteered to come over," he'll tell you, "and I'm proud that I came. If I had it all to do over I'd volunteer again . . ." and he adds with a grin, "Once."

Sgt. Taylor says hello to his parents and to nephew Tom who is staying with them. Taylor has been in Vietnam for 10 months.

Di An Vietnam, June 16, 1967

Perhaps the most important job in the war, next to that of the man actually fighting in the jungle, is the work of Captain Ed Bryson of Russellville.

Captain Bryson's job is "co-ordination". During the operation in the village of Hoa Nhut this morning, Bryson kept in touch constantly with every element of the 2nd Brigade, First Division. When some Vietnamese young men tried to break out of the surrounded village, Bryson was immediately notified; if artillery fire or aircraft are needed to support the troops, Bryson is the first to know.

In short, Ed Bryson is the lifeline for all the men in the jungle. For it is through him that the Division headquarters is informed of the progress of an entire operation.

Capt. Bryson's office today is a strong concrete block hut. The hut has over half a dozen two way radios, and four fans which hang from the ceiling, grudgingly shoving air from one corner to another.

But this place is relatievly comfortable. During the big operations, Cedar Falls and Junction City, this spring, Ed's office, which is called the Tactical Operations Center (TOC), looked more like an old fashioned wagon train circled up to ward off an attack by the Indians.

During the Junction City Operation, Ed was set up at a place called "Base Charlie", a locally infamous patch of mud that was under constant enemy mortar attack. The Vietcong know that knocking out Capt. Bryson's "office" will cripple an entire U.S. attack.

Yet, even under the tension and frantic pace of his work, Ed feels that a great deal of progress has been made since he arrived in Vietnam. "When I first arrived here," he says, "it took a full Division to open a short stretch of road for only one or two days. Then the moment the troops were gone the Vietcong came back in.

"But now we can open real lengthy stretches of highway for a long time with very few troops, and it will stay open with only occasional harrassment by the enemy. On Highway 13 at this time last year an entire batallion had been ambushed. Today the biggest thing that ever happens is four or five VC ambushing one lone vehicle."

Bryson says the morale of the troops here is "tremendous". They know what they are doing and why they are doing it. "If the men here, the troopers, the ones that really count didn't feel like we were doing the right thing here, their morale would be low—and it's not. And these guys are well-educated; no one is pulling the wool over their eyes."

Ed was born in Prescott, son of Mrs. E. B. Bryson and the late Mr. Bryson. But the twenty-six year old Arkansan was lured away to a new home town by a pretty young girl he met while they were at school at the University of Arkansas.

Now his wife, Mary Lou Davis Bryson is living in her home town of Russellville with their six year old son, Jim, and their daughter, Annette, three. Mary Lou is the daughter of Mrs. Thelma Davis and the late Mr. W. Garland Davis.

Cu Chi, June 18, 1967

Pfc. Birnes Penix of Wilmot wiped the sweat from his dark face. He chambered a round in his AR 15 rifle and shook his head to clear the roar of the helicopters from his ears. He then jumped from the chopper into the swirl of the dust and bullets that was supposed to be Charlie Company's landing zone. But it wasn't.

Face down in a rice paddy and with eyes straining to penetrate the jungle ahead, Penix experienced the confusion of battle. He recognized none of the people around him. He didn't know where he was, where his company was or what he should do. He did know there were snipers hiding in the trees ahead. He had been trained to react to that stimulus.

Penix was found five hours after the landing. His chopper had dropped him in the right place, but all the other helicopters in the assault from his company had dropped their troops in the wrong place, three miles away. Three miles is a long, long way in enemy territory, so Penix spent the rest of the day with Bravo Company.

Of course, Penix doesn't like any of it, but he says that it's the night patrolling that really bugs him. "Boy," he says, "I hate those things."

On Penix's second day in Vietnam he was sent out on a night ambush patrol. While changing positions in the blackness, his patrol crossed the lines of a group of South Vietnamese soldiers. Immediately the South Vietnamese sent up a flare, thinking the Vietcong were attacking.

"The flare went up right over my head," said Penix. "I was stretched out in the middle of the road—a perfect target— and right in front of me, maybe twenty feet away was a South

13

Vietnamese sighting a .50 calibre machine gun at me. That was a bad day."

Penix seems adjusted, reconciled, or whatever one calls the acceptance of the fact that he is in Vietnam to spend twelve months risking his life.

"When I first heard I was coming over, I really didn't want to come; but then I talked it over with my wife and my mother. Mother said, 'God is over there just like he is here in the United States, son; and he'll take care of you there just as he does here.'

"I don't blame the fellows at home for not wanting to come over; but our fathers fought just as we are fighting, and we owe it to them and to our children to be here. I think people over here deserve something better; they need something better. Mud houses, straw roofs, sleeping on dirt floors, drinking foul water—that's no way to live. People shouldn't live this."

Penix feels that he should live like that, for his year of duty anyway. "I felt bad, leaving my wife pregnant, but I felt like it was my duty. Now that I'm here I feel better about it."

Sitting in the sun on a rice paddy dike, with his grenades weighing down his sweat-soaked shirt and a can opener glistening under the band on his camouflaged helmet, Penix recalled the last time he had been summoned to the Company command post.

"The last time I was called in from the field was back in Fort Polk, on a day just as hot as this. That was real bad news. I was hoping this wasn't the same sort of thing."

On that day, Penix had been in his last hours of training in hand to hand combat. He was called to the company commander's office. His two-month-old son had died. "That was hard, real hard."

"But the Red Cross was effective. They deserve a compliment. Twelve hours after I got the news I was home, and they took care of the money for the burial."

Now Penix waits for the end of his tour of duty and thinks of his wife, Rosetta, and their six-month-old daughter, Vivian. "I miss them, and I miss all my old buddies from high school." Penix graduated from Slackle Grand High School in Wilmot in 1966.

"It seems like I've always been with the wolves", says Penix. "Our high school team was called the 'Wolves' and now I'm with the Wolfhounds." The Wolfhounds are a highly respected group of fighters, feared by the Vietcong.

"When I first got with the unit they kidded me a lot," says Penix, "I told them they would have to shape up. Back

14

in Arkansas, I said, we don't believe in being anything but Number One, so if you people can't be Number One then I just won't stay."

The Wolfhounds are definitely Number One around Cu Chi, and Penix likes his job and his companions, but says he will be glad to leave them both.

Before he joined the Army, Penix worked for Georgia Pacific in Crossett making plywood. He wants to go back there to work, wants to stay in Arkansas, but he says he is flirting with the idea of going out to California. "I have to take care of my family, and the pay is higher there." Then he adds again, "But I sure do like Arkansas."

Penix's nickname is "Rabbit", so named in highschool "because I was jumping all the time." He wants to thank his Boy Scout leaders fo rthe things they taught him, and his high school coach, Willie Parker, for the good physical conditioning he, Penix, received. And, finally, the Rabbit says "hi" to his good buddy, Will Clark, Jr.

June 20, 1967 (delayed)

Bob Higgins sat on the edge of his bunker south of the Bo Loi woods and looked over the barbed wire towards the fertile rice land of the Saigon River delta.

"I'm just looking forward to getting back to Atkins and working on the farm again. Pfc. Higgins' parents, Mr. and Mrs. R. H. Higgins of Atkins, have some good soybean land in the Atkins bottoms. The Vietnamese are mostly farmers, too, but watching them wade in their fields behind their wooden-yoked water buffaloes makes Bob say simply, "I'm not used to that kind of farming."

Higgins graduated from Atkins High School in 1963. He played right guard on the Red Devil's football team, and was president of the Beta Club and of his senior class. After farming with his dad for awhile he was called to the Army.

Bob took his basic training at Fort Polk, La., deep in the southern swamp land. "I'll say one thing for Fort Polk," grins Bob, "it's a great place to train before coming over here. It's sort of a little Vietnam."

Higgins has been on the line since he arrived in Vietnam in April. That means a twenty-four hour a day routine of patrols, ambushes, and filling sandbags to build bunkers. His company, Alpha Company of the 4th Battalion, 9th Infantry, 25th Division, has spent most of its time searching for the Vietcong in the Bo Loi woods thirty-five miles northwest of Saigon.

Not only must Higgins fight the VC in the woods, but

he must do battle with the stinging ants and the dense growth of trees and underbrush. "The red ants in there really tear you up!" says Bob. "I'd just as soon meet Charlie as run into those ants. We did well to make eighty yards an hour in there. We had to chop a path every foot of the way."

What's the life of an infantryman like? "I really don't know what to say; it's hard to put in words. A man just has to be over here to understand how bad it is. He'd just have to be here to understand.

Higgins sends his love to his wife, Judy, and his parents. Pfc. Higgins' brother-in-law, Dan Gipson, is also serving in Vietnam.

South of the Bo Loi Woods, June 20, 1967

On television they do it once a week, blasting across the desert sands, harassing the Germans . . . that's the "Rat Patrol". Here in Vietnam, just south of the infamous Bo Loi woods, Sgt. Clarence James Gray of Little Rock, leads six men and two gun Jeeps into this daily exercise in organized insanity.

Sgt. Gray, with the Fourth Battalion, Ninth Infantry, has been blasting along the jungle trails of Vietnam at 70 miles an hour for most of his eleven months here. His life depends on how well he keeps his men, their jeeps, and their two M-60 machine guns operating.

Perhaps more so than any other unit in Vietnam Sgt. Gray's team is completely, totally interdependent. The jeep must not stall; the gun must not jam; the gunner must return fire directly at the enemy; the driver must not falter. And Sgt. Gray must be able to give the right orders, and at the right time under heavy fire.

Outwardly, Gray's jeep is a standard, dust-covered, militarily drab, unexciting hulk. The only distinguishing feature on the vehicle is the long, sleek snout of Gray's "Baby", "Best Friend", Mother", "Father", "Lover" and "Protector": the M-60 machine gun.

The gun sits godlike on its dust-covered altar, and seems to glow under the admiring smile and caresses of "its people." Under the hood of the "altar" sits an engine as clean and well-tuned as any that ever took the track at Indianapolis. The driver of this deformed racer is racing for his life when he gets behind the wheel.

The "Recondo" teams, as they are often called, seek out the enemy, they precede and follow all convoys to prevent sneak attacks. They continually patrol roads that are dangerous even

17

for tanks and heavily armored vehicles to travel. They look for Vietcong tax collectors, road blocks, snipers and mines, and they usually find them—the hard way.

The floor of the jeeps are covered with sandbags to absorb some of the blast if they do hit a mine. But as Gray says, "The best thing we can do is just try and drive so fast that the mine will explode behind us."

Mines have exploded in front of Gray, and behind him; snipers have fired all around him, but so far he has been untouched. The hardest part of his existence at this point is trying to make these last thirty days disappear. They compose his final month in Vietnam.

"When I first arrived I was scared, real scared," says Gray; "but I got over that in a couple of weeks. I was just so busy that I didn't have time to worry."

With only thirty days left now, Gray is officially a "short timer". "Once you start getting kind of short, you start getting kind of scared . . . all over again." And time drags. "The first six months went real fast; but then, man, they don't move at all."

Vietnam isn't all bad in Sgt. Gray's opinion—just mostly bad. "Actually, Vietnam might be a nice place to live if there weren't a war. Some of the people are real nice and friendly.

"There's a papasan down in Trang Bang who gives us a big bowl of noodle soup and a big glass of rum with a little tiny bit of coke in it every time we come to town. He won't let us pay him for it either, no matter how many of us come, or how often we come. He even gets mad if we try and pay him. He just stands there and smiles and brings another bowl of soup.

"They seem amazed that we are so big," says the six-foot Negro. "Most of the Vietnamese get a kick out of my skin too. They think the color will rub off. The kids come over and rub at it and pinch it, then laugh like crazy."

But as much as Gray likes the people, the rest of the country leaves him cold, hot, sweaty, chilled, and scared. It is standard operating procedure here to shake your boots each morning before putting them on. Most anything may fall out. Black scorpions as large as a good iron frying pan cruise through the grass looking for whatever it is they eat.

"And don't leave out the red ants," says Gray. "Those red ants are something else." Gray and all the men here sound somewhat awed when they speak of the ants. "You get all swelled up from them. There's just no comparison, not at all. Except, maybe, well maybe, yeah! Like a rattlesnake bite, that's pretty close.!"

All of his buddies have pretty good morale, Gray feels. But

he gets angry when he speaks of the guys who never get any mail from home. "This is the time you need to hear from someone," says Gray. "All you can do when you get over here is count the days until you can go home, and you've got to feel that someone back home cares about you. The married guys have it real tough. One guy in my squad hasn't had a letter from his wife in over a month. He's sending her all that dough home; the very least she could do is mail him a letter once a week.

"Of course some guys come over and think they are real rugged, and don't give a damn, don't care. But they get over that pretty quick. A guy here just has to have someone who cares for him and he needs to care for someone."

Clarence's mother, Mrs. Louise Gray of Little Rock, has three sons in the service right now. One of Clarence's brothers, Lawrence, was stationed in Da Nang for a year and Clarence went up to visit with him a few months ago.

Another brother, Richmond, is in the Air Force. But Clarence is especially proud of his youngest brother, Willie, a student at J. C. Cook Junior High School.

Gray speaks of Willie with obvious affection: "He's real smart. He works hard an dhe wants to be a doctor. He's going to do fine in life. He's real smart."

As soon as he gets home, Gray wants two things which are the eternal dreams of any soldier at war: "A good home-cooked meal and a good, hot bath in a bath tub." And, Mrs. Gray, Clarence says he wants that meal to include "collard greens, ham hock, butter milk, black-eyed peas, and corn bread."

The nineteen-year-old Gray graduated from Biscoe High School in 1963, where he played on the basketball team. He worked part time at the University of Arkansas Medical Center in Little Rock and at the John R. Jernigan Deep Rock Service Station while he was in school. After he leaves the service Clarence hopes to attend college on the GI bill and get a degree in Business Administration. Then he would like to stay in Arkansas if he can find a good job there.

Two years ago the "Iron Triangle" thirty miles northwest of Saigon was a Vietcong stronghold never trespassed upon by either government or United States soldiers. The dense wooded area received its name long ago from its triangular shape, and from the severe defeats suffered there by rash generals who had sometimes sought to penetrat its unblighted borders.

Today, PFC Ernest L. (Mac) McCain of Searcy, Rosebud, Booneville and Malvern makes his home inside a 13 ton armored personnel carrier that butts its way in and out of every inch of this former Vietcong sanctuary.

The 25-year-old son of Mr. and Mrs. E. L. McCain Sr. and grandson of Mr. W. F. Hays of Russell, Mac has seen half of his tour of duty in Vietnam as a driver of APC 24, Troop B, 3rd Squadron, 4th Cavalry, 25th Division.

Flying over Mac's present "stomping grounds," the scarred earth below offers striking testimony of the extent of U.S. operations inside the Triangle. Deep bomb craters are seen throughout the woods. The fresh craters show a face of wet brown mud, outlined by the torn rubber trees, with their yellow trunks dripping white blood. The older craters have filled with clear blue rainwater, lovely lagoons in a lonely land.

Mac's cavalry unit is accessible only by helicopter. Flying low and erratically, the chopper pilots often must break through thick fog to find the constantly changing camping grounds of the cavalry. At seven o'clock in the morning, Mac's unit looks like the old covered wagon train: circled up, cook fires glowing, repairs under way, and the enemy hiding in the thick brush a few hundred yards away.

On the morning of Wednesday, June 21, Mac was worknig furiously to replace one of the tracks on his APC. Though the sun was not yet over the trees and the fog was clinging to him, his slender, muscled back was streaked with a muddy early-morning sweat.

This Wednesday was to have been devoted to repair work before his troop of APC's and tanks went back into the jungle around them. But Dennis Graff, the cheery, chubby sergeant from Syracuse, Indiana who commands APC 24 had just stomped back through the wet grass of the camp to inform his four-man crew that a VC defector had reported the location of the Vietcong MR 4 Regimental Headquarters protected by three squads of Communists. The location was only a one hour ride from where the "three quarter," as it is called, was camped.

Graff had told his crew to "mount up" and be ready to move out within fifteen minutes. So Mac was trying to replace the track that he had earlier removed and hoped to repair during the planned respite in their fighting. With the track back on, Mac stowed his tools inside his machine and climbed into the "saddle."

Looking for all the world like a troop of blue-coated cavalry preparing to march through the western badlands, Mac and his mates mounted their armored animals, started the great engines that sit to the right of the drivers' stations, talked to their gears, then placed their "tracks" into line, moving off through the ordered trees of the rubber plantation to the south.

Driving an armored personnel carrier properly is as difficult as flying a helicopter under fire. Mac stands rather than sits, using both hands to control the speed of the two tracks on his machine and the direction of the thirteen ton creature. He was not "on point" today, a fact for which he was profoundly grateful, so the threat of setting off a "pressure mine" was not so great. Yet, Mac followed precisely in the tracks of the carriers in front of him. Even a slight deviation from the already tested soil the preceding track had churned might be death for him and his crew. Only when the cavalcade stopped for a moment and each carrier nosed about ten yards off the path in alternating directions, did Mac have to cross new ground. But when the march was resumed he carefully backed over his old tracks into line rather than swinging around in a circle to regain the line of march.

Within a few minutes the tracks moved out of the rubber trees and began speeding along at a faster pace down the side of a small, rotting asphalt road.

The vehicles never actually touched the surface of the road except to cross it. Mac generally keeps his track about thirty yards back of the preceding track. Even that may not be far enough away to avoid the thousands, tens of thousands of mines that have been planted along the highway for the last twenty years.

Burned out bunkers of dirt and concrete, many with metal beams, most containing well protected machine gun ports, stand lifeless where once they were a bustling center of Communist activity grinding out propaganda leaflets, making weapons, providing hospital care for wounded Vietcong, collecting taxes from travelers seeking to drive to Tay Ninh near the Cambodian border—in general sitting as an arrogant and defiant blockade across an important artery leading into Saigon.

Up and down this road, the Vietcong moved troops, weapons, supplies, and infiltrators. The Government of Vietnam was never able to challenge the position.

Bombs did little damage to the bunkers; armored convoys attempting to move on the camp from Saigon were ambushed enroute.

Today the Communists have been partially routed from this position by Mac and the three-quarter cavalry. Yet, just a few miles further up the road another camp had been established: this one merely moved further into the jungle and built more solidly.

As Mac moved towards that camp last week, tension in his track mounted. Sgt. Graff kept his finger only a fraction of an inch from the trigger of the 50 calibre machine gun that is the major weapon of the APC. Mac tried to keep the sweat on his glasses lens from obscuring his vision; the other three members of the crew sat around the turrent of the track.

Shirtless except for the brown fibreglass-packed flak jacket, they stared out from under their camouflaged helmets, took their M-16 rifles off 'safe', and hoped no ambush was planned, hoped no sniper would risk doing battle with the 50 calibres in order to hit one of the unprotected men riding atop the tracks.

Seldom do the men stay inside the track when it is on the move. It's not an uncomfortable place. Fairly cool, protected from the sun, and from sniper bullets, the men could sleep inside the tracks. But each of them knows that should their track be hit by the RPG II, a Russian antitank weapon similar to a bazooka, being inside would mean death.

Earlier Mac had looked over several of the tracks that had been hit by RPG fire in the last few days. The entry point of the missle is a small but ugly round hole punched through the thick metal sides of the track; around this hole are deep gashes in the track's iron-grey flanks. The metal looks as though it was wax and had been melted by slashes with a red hot iron rod.

Once having penetrated the track and found its way inside, the RPG explodes. Everything inside the track is destroyed by the concussion and countless pieces of shrapnel. Thus the crew of the track rides on top and risks sniper fire.

As Mac drove into the outer perimeter of the camp there was a sudden sharp "bang" twenty yards behind him. A mine! The sharp sick smell of cordite filled the air and an ugly black and grey cloud leaped into the air beside the tank following Mac. Immediately the men on the tracks sprayed both sides of the road with machine gun fire.

It was clear that the mine had been "command" detonated, that is set off by someone hiding in the bushes watching the tracks go by. The VC had decided to try and knock out the tank, a welcome mistake. It was a big mine and would have destroyed APC 24, but the seven-to-ten inch thick sides of the tank absorbed the blast. The tank joined the machine gun fire with one blast from its cannon. The cavalry again started moving.

Fear flourished under the hot sun; the top of APC 24 was covered with the sweat from the men and the empty shell cases from their weapons.

Mac turned Number 24 to the right and faced it into the jungle. Track No. 23 moved in front of him and then they roared into the solid front of foliage, while all down the line of jungle, for a mile in each direction, other tracks also advanced into the VC fortification.

Number 23 was immobilized instantly, not by the VC, but by thousands of red ants that had been shaken loose from one of the trees. They swarmed over the driver, gunner, and crew of the tank. There was nothing to do but discard weapons, back out, and try and rid themselves of the stinging beasts.

Over ten yards and another thrust took Mac out of the sun and into the dark closeness of the jungle. Although the APC's were only yards apart Mac could barely see the track in front of him. He stopped No. 24 and the three man crew jumped off to begin their duty: going on foot and on their knees into the jungle around them, moving into a wet hell of agony. The Vietcong have booby traps that do unspeakable things to a man. The jungle is so thick that a VC may reach from behind a tree and slit a man's throat without being seen by other soldiers all around him.

In the jungle the bunkers were found, searched and explosives laid to destroy them. Mac sat on top of his track and talked of the mine explosion. "I've seen lots of mines go off in front of me, but that's the first one I've seen go off behind me. Charlie just can't resist trying to knock off one of those tanks."

Mac and Graff took out their 'c-rations', tore a chunk of the white c-4 explosive from its block and set fire to it to heat their rations.

The 'c's' contain peaches, apricots, and pears; also crackers, cheddar cheese, ham and limabeans (highly unpopular), chicken noodles, meat and potatoes, and 'tropic' chocolate, reminiscent of eating soft brown chalk.

Sporadic fire and grenade explosions came from the bushes around them, as Graff and Mac ate and laughed about the time a man on the machine gun was firing during a night attack and lost his teeth.

"He was standing up there, spraying fifty calibre bullets all over the woods," said Mac. "Then he suddenly stopped. 'My teeth! Where are my teeth?' he was yelling. We looked for them the next morning. The gun had vibrated him so much the teeth had fallen out into the bullet can." They both were in good spirits, trying to laugh off the tightness in their nerves.

Then the rain began. The jungle floor around them became a wide, flat pool of water. Temperatures dropped ten to twenty degrees within an hour; a wind kicked up and the crew crawled out of the jungle cursing the cold.

By about five-thirty in the afternoon, Mac was searching his way back to the road. Two of the crew members stood over the exhaust grille, trying to catch some warmth from the engine before the cold wind stole it.

Track 29 fell in behind Mac who was leading the group now. The mud was stubbornly, crippling trick, and the tracks were having a difficult time moving. Soon Mac was stuck in a shallow depression. Track 29 pulled in front; Mac roared out of the ditch and they resumed moving to the camp area.

Within ten yards Track 29 was covered with the black cloud of another mine explosion. Shrapnel bounced off the flak jackets and helmets of Mac's crew. Men from Track 29 fell to the ground, rolled over, tried to stand, then fell again.

Under the left side of No. 29 was a six foot wide by six foot deep crater. The track on 29 had been blown apart. Mac and Graff stared grimly while the medic teams rushed to the aid of the wounded men. Simultaneously Mac and Graff whispered, "That should have been us." Graff's radio crackled and he pulled his track around 29 and continued on to the camping grounds.

It was dark by the time Mac was back in position. He lifted himself out of his seat, by the edges of the periscopes that give the driver a view when he is under attack.

"That was a typical day," he said.

The black hulks of the other tracks loomed in the darkness and cook fires were started. Three more mine explosions within the perimeter of the tracks affirmed Mac's earlier guess that they were spending the night in a mine field.

One man began walking in concentric circles to the center

of the camp, searching with a mine sweeper for anymore of the deadly devices. Other men stood over the exhausts of the idling engines trying to dry their clothes. A shivering Mac picked his way down a rut cut by one of the tracks to the chow track. There a hot meal, brought in by helicopter a few moments before, was being served. With his orange, meat and potatoes, Mac sat by the exhaust to dry and eat.

Mac is a long way from Arkansas in every respect. He sat there and talked of his days at Arkansas Tech, of his degree in Engineering, of his hopes for the future and his plans for using the leave time he will have accumulated. "When I get home I'm just going to take it easy for about thirty days and see all of my people," he said.

An artillery piece blasts in the distance, throwing its singing shell over the track and into the jungle a thousand yards away. "I don't think about the mine or the RPG's . . . if I did, if any of us did, we couldn't stand it. I don't really think about anything while I'm here."

Mac stood guard for two hours that night before crawling inside Track 24 and curling up half on top of his driver's seat and half on a pile of flak jackets and c-rations. The noise and concussion from the bombing outside, the glow of the flares, the constant small blasts from grenades fired into the dark to harass any attempted VC infiltration, all failed to awaken him.

At dawn Mac mounted up again, watched two companies of infantrymen, landed by helicopter, move on foot into the jungle, listened to the gunfire for thirty minutes, then got his new orders from Sgt. Graff and swung back into line. Teeth clenched, eyes red, covered with sweat and mud and fear Mac McCain started another "typical day."

In March 1965, the United States Marines landed on the sandy wastes at Danang, Vietnam. In May, 1965, Tommy C. Thompson, son of Mr. and Mrs. E. C. Thompson of Little Rock, graduated from Hall High School. Not long after that, Tommy married his high school sweetheart, Barbara Hanns. On January, 1967, Barbara gave birth to their daughter, Donna. Day before yesterday Tommy received his second purple heart in Vietnam.

Since he gets shot at almost every day, Tommy might receive his third purple heart, and an automatic free ticket home, at any time. "And I'd like to have it," he says, "but only if it's just a little scratch that gives it to me . . . not like the first time; I don't want that to happen again."

The first time was in Operation Union last April. Dropping through the clouds and swinging across a rice paddy on a mission to evacuate a wounded Marine, Tommy's helicopter was the target for every enemy machine gun surviving the furious poundings of jet fighters that had supposedly "softened up the area" before Calvin's chopper went in.

Many enemy guns had survived. One of those sent a .30-calibre bullet slashing through the side of the helicopter; the amorphous mass tore through Tommy's fibreglass flak jacket down low on this side, carved a ragged path up his rib cage, and lodged itself under his arm. He was on the hospital ship "Sanctuary" for three weeks with that wound.

On June 29, he was lifting a group of Marines out of a 'hot' landing zone when the second wound came. The air was thick with bullets; one Marine was hit in the leg as he crawled into the chopper. Tom got it in the neck. As he returned fire, a bullet slashed at the back of his neck, splattering him with shrapnel. He spent two hours at the infirmary with that wound. Neck covered with iodine, he was back at his job the same day.

Tommy's work day runs from twelve to fifteen hours. His work week is all week. His office is at the window of a UH 34 D Marine Helicopter. His tools consist of a 7.6 calibre machine gun and a set of iron-hard nerves. Sometimes he is able to relax. "At night we just circle around mostly and all I have to do is watch for mortar flashes below." But during the day: "I'm always watching for someone who's trying to 'ding' me."

The UD 34 helicopter is about fifteen paces long with a great bulbous nose and floppy dragonfly like wings. The green machine does indeed resemble a dragonfly or a grasshopper. It's skin is patched here and there: small and large, usually square, the patches are a litle more yellow than the rest of the aircraft; but there are so many patches in Helicopter Number 20 that it will soon be hard to tell which color was the original.

Inside, two thick masses of wire wrapped in white, oil-smudged plastic slip snake-like out of the tail over the heads of the two gunners, through the stomach of the machine and into its cockpit. From the stomach, only the legs of the pilots are visible in the cockpit. Two pairs of legs with boots dangle, disembodied, as would the legs of a man on the gallows. They jerk irregularly, manuvering the foot controls.

Tommy sits on what is, essentially, a kitchen chair. Bolted to the floor, the chair is draped with flak jackets. Two over the back to ward off bullets from that direction; one under the chair and one Tom sits on for protection from fire entering the sofe underbelly of the machine. Two jackets are wadded, crammed and wrapped, stuffed into a small crevice by his left arm.

Facing the pilot, Tom sits on the left side of Number 20 and must protect against all attacks from that direction. He carries a wooden handled thirty-eight revolver on his hip. His flight uniform is all zippers, pockets, and dirt.

Tommy's grey-back plastic flight helmet has his initials emblazoned in yellow on the visor protector. In rain or dust, or when looking into the sun he pulls the green-tinted visor down out of the helmet. So positioned, only the base of his chin, and his mouth are visible. The rest of his face is green, opaque plastic. On his hands he wears soft leather kid gloves. They fit tightly, absorbing some of the vibration of the machine gun and preventing his sweat-soaked hands from slipping as he reloads.

On the afternoon of June 30, Tommy made four trips in his chopper. They were run of the mill, except for the fact they weren't fired on that day. On the first two trips Number 20 carried a load of food and supplies for Marines in the field.

Tommy and his co-gunner loaded the boxes on board: case after case of 'c' rations stored in cardboard brown boxes and stenciled in military fashion "Meal—Combat—Individual."

There were oranges from the Florida citrus growers association, Washington State apples packed in a white box with a red-faced "Mr. Apple" wearing a mortar board smiling from its side. There was grape juice from Pennsylvania, grapefruit juice from California, pineapple juice from Hawaii, and grey bags filled with thousands of small plastic, saccharine-type bottles of mosquito repellant.

The grasshopper bounced into the air with its cargo, went up to twenty-five hundred feet and then dropped rock-like through the air, careening from cloud to cloud to avoid bullets from below.

The moment it touched down, Tom unstrapped his safety belt (a loose belt whose purpose is not to hold the gunner in his seat, but to keep him from being sucked out the open door of the chopper). Panic seemed to hold sway as he and his co-gunner hurled the cargo out the door. Too long on the ground in a forward area invites destruction for the helicopter and its crew.

Green visors flashing in the sun, heads bent, bodies swaying under the load, the blond-haired Little Rock boy turned into a sort of man-ant-parasite flushing the stomach of his grasshopper home.

As the last box hit the ground, Number 20 began clawing at the air with its floppy rotor blades and dodging into the clouds. Having regained altitude, Tommy looked at the crushed orange on the floor of the chopper; its juice had splashed across his boots, and now was gathering a little colored pool on the floor and rippling from the vibrations of the flight. Perhaps it reminded young Tommy of the blood of the young Marine he had hauled out of a rice paddy last week. Both his legs had been blown off, "one below the knee and one above the knee" by a booby trap. Or perhaps it reminded him simply of the early mornings before school, or in early marriage, when the orange juice came ice-cold and comforting to his lips, and why it could not be like that now. Perhaps it passed by him completely unnoticed, as many small, reflective things in the most lethal, lashing moments of maneuvering in a forward area.

As Number 20 was reloaded for another trip, Tommy sat and chewed one of the apples, oblivious to the dust that had settled on it; unconscious of the sweat that beaded on his sun-burned nose and across his upper lip that needs only an occasional shaving.

Outside a Marine lay asleep under a water carrier. Tommy threw the apple core out the door as a man would dash an empty champagne glass into the fireplace. He sat, letting the sounds of his helicopter wash over him. Far too much noise to talk, he listened to the roar of the engine, the whine of the rotor blades slashing at the dust-laden air, the wind seeking to find a way under his heavy flak jacket to cool him, the nervous crackle of his headset: these are the "sounds of silence" in a helicopter.

Another trip out; this time the chopper settled in an open rice paddy while a patrol of Marines kept their rifles pointed at the surrounding fields. Three blindfolded Vietnamese were led to the helicopter. Tommy pulled them inside and then fell back to his seat as the chopper lifted off.

The three men were naked but for white pajama bottoms tied with string. Their blindfolds had once been their shirts. Their feet were mud-caked and calloused.

One man freed his hands. Tommy jumped on him; then another passenger helped. The prisoner trembled violently, unable to see, only able to feel the wind rushing past him and recall the stories he had heard of prisoners being thrown from such helicopters.

The prisoners sat very still on that battered, screw-studded, paint peeling, aluminum helicopter floor. Each man was tagged as would be a package in parcel post. The tags had each man's name, age, and circumstances of capture. One was thirty-five years of age. He had been found hiding in a hedge row and had tried to run away from the Marines that caught him. Another was twenty-seven; he and the third, who was thirty-five, were reported by a Vietnamese civilian to have been "carrying a pack".

A hard rain forced Number 20 back to base for an hour, and Tommy had a cold soft drink at "Snoopy's Hangout", the squadron snackbar. He lit a cigarette with an engraved lighter picturing Snoopy, scarf blowing in the breeze, mounted on his bullet-riddled "sopwith camel." The squadron mascot, "Snoopy", who looks as much like the cartoon character as any dog in the world possibly could, walked from handpat to handpat, to ear scratching.

Having been asked what kind of dog he was, Tommy replied, "I don't know. Vietnamese is all I could say. He rides a lot of the choppers; he'll sleep right through a fire fight out there."

Ask Tommy what he misses the most other than his wife and family and he'll say immediately, "Clean sheets . . . or, for that matter, sheets period." He watches television for relaxation.

Tommy loves flying, even with the danger he faces in Vietnam. "The Medevacs are the best part of the job," he says. "When we can go bring out someone that's been hit, then I feel like I've accomplished something, helped someone."

The rain stopped and Tommy went out for his last trip of the day: lifting a Vietnamese soldier with a leg wound out of a battle and into a hospital and temporary safety. "It feels so good to be able to help a buddy."

The nineteen-year-old Calvin has a brother, Johnny, 20, who is in the Air Force and stationed in Texarkana. His married sister, Florine Barnett lives in St. Louis. His wife is the daughter of Mrs. W. D. Hanns and the late Mr. Hanns. Tommy is the son of Mr. and Mrs. E. C. Calvin, Little Rock. Tommy and his wife have a daughter, Donna, born this past January.

Da Nang, June 30, 1967

Ever since he left Arkansas State Teachers College at Conway in 1942, Sam Beal has been in Marine Corps Aviation, and he has grown along with it. "I started as a fighter pilot flying the Corsair and as a carrier pilot in World War Two," he says. "Then I was a jet pilot in Korea; now I'm a helicopter pilot in Vietnam." The 1940 graduate of Little Rock High School has flown all kinds of aircraft: day and night fighters, transports, and helicopters. However, at this point in his military career Colonel Beal's rank prevents his spending as much time in the cockpit as he would like. He is now commanding officer of Heavy Marine Helicopter wing 463. His major difficulty, he says, is maintaining an efficient organization and keeping his aircraft and his men in working condition.

"Our men are working twelve to fifteen hours a day in this dust and heat. They leave early each morning, and have to stay in that 'greenhouse' cockpit all day long." "These are the worst possible conditions for the helicopters to have to work in," he says.

The heated air is thin and cuts down engine efficiency and the dust wears the engine rapidly. "We do have something that we hope will reduce the dust problem. We call it the Engine Air Particle Separator and it acts, says Beal, like a filter. As the dust and air are sucked towards the engine the air is swirled down a series of tubes. The centrifugal force throws the dust out the side and lets the clean air through."

Colonel Beal's helicopters are really the first of their kind in the country. Four were brought in for testing purposes before he arrived but his unit of 22 CH 53A Sea Stallions was the first operational group in the country. The Sea Stallion is the largest, fastest, strongest helicopter in the free world. "Its speed is in excess of 200 miles per hour and its load carrying capacity has been tested with as much as 15,000 pounds," says Beal. "And we regularly lift loads of 12,000 pounds."

This is Colonel Beal's second tour of duty in Vietnam. He

was here in 1964; in fact he left just three years ago this June. "At that time there were only five hundred Marines in Vietnam and one helicopter squadron. Our major job was supporting the Vietnamese Army and supplying the United States Special Forces camps."

Today he obviously can see a lot of changes in the war. The one he is most concerned with is the change in the enemy strength. "They have more sophisticated weapons now and more high calibre weapons." And of course that means they can knock more of his helicopters out of the sky.

He's seen a tremendous change in Marine aviation in his twenty-five years in the sky. "Probably the majority of Marine aircraft today are helicopters; and where we used to use them only to transport men and supplies now they are used as close support aircraft. They are gunships hovering at the sight of the battle and providing a major source of firepower."

In the miserably-thick jungles, with dense over-growth 8 to 10 feet above the ground, it is often difficult to see marching Vietcong. With clearings patched briefly here and there, it is nearly impossible to land most aircraft. The airplane can bomb, but is often too fast to scout and land. Only the helicopter can fight the searching, shooting, quick landing and quicker leaving air war required in the Vietnamese forests.

Looking out at the sandy stretches of the Da Nang airfield, Beal says, "This time next summer I'll be in Hot Springs on the lake with my wife and family. Beal met his wife, the former Billie Shryrock of Conway, granddaughter of Mrs. Pearl Sauls of Conway, and niece of Mrs. Bernice Smith, Dean of Women at Henderson; while she was a student with him in Conway. She was studying at Hendrix. In the summer Billie, and their three children, Karen, who is a senior majoring in psychology at the University of Arkansas, and Ann, and Jim join him for "fishing, waterskiing, and boating." Colonel Beal is the brother of Robert K. Beal, a Vice President of Rector-Phillips-Morse and Mrs. Elizabeth Mayhew, both of Little Rock.

Phu Bai, Vietnam, July 5, 1967

For the hundreds of combat Marines who stop over at the Phu Bai airport, the first thing they see when they step outside for a breath of air is a large Arkansas state flag flying over the 'home' of Lance Corporal David McLaughlin of Ft. Smith. Now flying at the end of a long stick of bamboo stuck through the roof of his sandbagged mortar shelter, the big red flag came to David within ten days after he wrote Governor Rockefeller that he would like to have one.

McLaughlin, 19, the son of Mr. and Mrs. Dale V. McLaughlin, Fort Smith, is one of the thousands of "support" troops that back up the "line" companies and help them do their jobs. David does his part by feeding the doctors and corpsmen who care for the wounded. "I'm happy I've been lucky enough to be stationed in 'the rear' ", says David.

In Vietnam, of course, there is no real "rear". Everyone in the country is threatened with the danger of attack at any time. David's area was mortared on the 28th of April. "But none of them came close", he says. How far away is "not close"? "Oh, way over on the airfield," says David. "Way over on the airfield," is all of fifty yards from his bunk. For the last week, while bitter fighting raged twenty miles north of his position, David has been under orders to carry his combat gear with him every place he goes. "Even to the movies and the bathroom!"

David left Subiaco Academy in 1965 to join the Marines; they promptly sent him off to Baking School. And today, David can make and cook "sweet" doughs, "sour" doughs, and "in between" doughs. "We learned to operate about forty different kinds of ovens for use in the field and at base. They even taught a course in 'basic cake decorations' ", laughs McLaughlin.

On his time off, David goes with the "Medical Civic Action

Pacification" teams (MEDCAPs). He's been able to get into many of the small villages and towns in the area as a result and is slowly picking up some of the Vietnamese language. As for the people: "I like them. They're not bad people at all. I'm even starting to eat some of their food."

The food he cooks is received in the standard time approved military fashion: "With a lot of grumbling". But the little complaints don't bother him. "As long as we get the usual kidding about the food we feel fine. We'd be worried only if everyone clammed up all of a sudden. Then we would know something was wrong for sure."

Despite the quick return of the flag he asked for, David says the mail service has been "all screwed up lately." "That's all the guys have to look forward to; and so when it gets fouled up they get all depressed."

In addition to the letters David receives from home, his family sends him the **Southwest American** and **Ft. Smith Times Record**. "It's great to be able to keep up with what's happening in the state," he says. David plans to stay in Arkansas and looks forward to getting out of the service in February of '69 so he can start college at the University of Arkansas and work on his degree in education. "Then I'd like to come back to Ft. Smith and teach."

Living in a wooden hut with a corrugated tin roof, David has boxed off his bed with old ammo crates . . . sort of his "office". On the shelf over his bed is a long line of books. Outside is a sea of two-inch-deep dust that is blown through his hut constantly by the rotors of the aircraft across the way. A huge power generator almost drowns out all attempts to listen to the radio or even talk. "I miss the comforts of home", he admits. Most of all he misses his folks and his sister, Yvonne and also his girl, Shirley Smith of Russellville.

"Yeah," says the nineteen-year-old Marine, "I really miss Shirley".

Phu Bai, Vietnam, July 6, 1967

Lance Corporal Lloyd E. Parker, Jr., 19, of Melbourne has been in Vietnam for seven months. He feels like he has personally walked across every inch of land between Da Nang and the Demilitarized Zone; and he spends about eight hours a night now walking back and forth over a three square mile area outside Phu Bai, where his job is radioman with the Third Marine Division.

Parker's platoon is presently providing security for the Phu Bai area, accomplished by constant night patrols and ambushes.

On July 3, "Junior", as he is called, was on a patrol that ambushed fifteen Vietcong. "They left four bodies behind," said Parker, "but it happened so fast I didn't really see it. Most of us were asleep actually, when one of our men saw them coming. He opened fire with his .45 pistol; then we woke up and used our rifles. I guess we must have confused them a little, starting out with the .45 that way."

Parker's worst experience came on Operation Hickory on May 25 at Hill 117 along the DMZ. "We were set up on top of the hill, all dug in, when we started receiving mortar fire at about four in the morning. I was asleep outside my hole when I first heard "the tubes". Way off in the distance I could hear them firing; but I was bushed and really didn't want to move. Then a buddy reached out and pulled me into the hole with him just as the shells started landing."

It is an age-old story of war: in the late, lonely night, with muscles tired and aching, mind weary from war and waiting, the exhaustion leaves the soldier sometimes indifferent. The danger seems a far-away fantasy; the body does not want to move, the mind cannot force it to. The conscious instinct of self-survival is pushed away by a semi-conscious, somniac stupor, and perhaps, in such submissive moments, a self-pitying subconscious dream that perhaps unheard, unfelt explosion will end it all: the dragging, deadly days, the long, lonely, lethal nights.

Parker was lucky; a buddy was there to save him. Some, many, are not so lucky.

"It was dark and we couldn't see a thing except the flashes when the shells hit," said Parker. "There were about thirty rounds fired at us. Things quieted down for about an hour; then Charlie ambushed our ambush patrol as it was returning to the camp area. The commander sent down the third platoon to relieve them; but they got hit too. So, finally, it was our turn.

"We started out just as the sun was coming up. We were moving down a pretty steep hill and skirting an overgrown rice paddy. Just as we reached the tree line they opened up on us with automatic weapons fire — thirty calibre stuff. The lieutenant got it right away. He took about eight rounds of machinegun fire right across his chest. Then the sergeant took over and pulled us a little ways back up the hill. Our platoon alone had taken three dead and four wounded."

The sergeant held us on the hill for awhile so we could be resupplied with ammunition and food. The artillery blasted away at Charlie while we were resting.

"About two in the afternoon we decided to try again. We

hit them, but the artillery fire hadn't been able to dent the bunkers they were in. They had three 30 calibres that I saw."

"Who was killed on that time down?" Junior called across the bunks to one of his buddies.

"Well," said the other, "there was McCombs and Jeeter."

"Didn't Parker get it too?" asked a third.

"Yeah, and so did Wilson; no, that was later."

"Anyway," continued Junior, "I was assigned to an m-79 grenade launcher then. I tried to use it but the brush was so thick that the grenades exploded before they could really get close to the target. So, back up that hill we went again."

"The next morning the c/o gave us orders to try one more time. The captain and a lot of brass went out to fly over the area in their chopper to see what the situation was. The minute they got close the chopper was shot down. The Captain was killed. The Colonel got a fifty calibre round in his leg and shoulder. The Major and the pilot got hurt too. So after that, they just gave us orders to get the heck out of there. And we were glad to go."

Parker told his story without emotion. After seven months of such operations, he's used to them. He would destroy himself if he let himself waste emotions on every incident he has been through.

He does get upset about the draft card burners at home. "If anyone has to come over, everyone should have to. I guess the war is good for the Vietnamese who favor Saigon. I'm not really sure it's good for the United States. But I'm here and I don't like the idea of these demonstrators who feel like they can get out of doing what I'm having to do."

Junior tapped some ashes off his cigarette into the top of a Pabst beer can that had the top peeled back. He looked at the mess gear and rifles hanging from the ceiling of his "hootch" and at his friends, sleeping, cleaning their weapons, writing letters.

"I just want to get home where it's peaceful and do some fishing up at Lake Norfolk," said Junior. "That's all I want to do."

Parker is the son of Mr. and Mrs. Lloyd Parker, Sr. of Melbourne. He is a 1965 graduate of Melbourne High School.

Just over twenty years ago, Edward M. Crowley, Sr. was at war in the Solomon Islands; his job was with Marine Corps artillery. In July, of this year, his son, Marine Corps Sergeant Mike Crowley, was at war in Khe Sanh, Vietnam; and his job was with Marine artillery. Mike was the assistant operations chief at the Fire Support Coordination Center at the outpost of Khe Sanh. He and a Lieutenant shared the responsibility and the duty hours of making sure that when the dozens of artillery pieces at Khe Sanh open fire it was the enemy at which they fired and not their own men.

In every war the man on the line has feared the short round. That is, one of his own artillery or mortar shells which lands on him instead of the enemy. It can happen because of poor aiming, lack of sufficient powder in the shell or just because someone has called in the artillery at the wrong place. Mike saw to it that it wouldn't happen to the 2,500 Marines for whom he was responsible. Mike's office was deep inside a heavily sandbagged bunker set in the ground at the base of a semicircle of high mountains that look north to the DMZ 15 miles away. Some of those hills have famous and bloody names . . . Hill 881 and Hill 886, for example.

Ground action in the immediate area had slacked off in the first weeks of July, but could have begun again at anytime. At least once a night the men at the camp race from their tents and dive face first into the dirt holes that dot the mile wide perimeter. The North Vietnamese may drive them to these holes with artillery, mortars or rockets. Some men don't get there in time; Sgt. Crowley's tent, where he sometimes sits and talks with buddies in the hot close atmosphere, has many large holes from the shrapnel. They let through ragged shafts of light that dance and waver as they slide through the dust laden

36

air. "I stay in my bunker all the time," says Mike. Those that don't, wait for shipment out in a small, sixteen foot by sixteen foot square building with a corrugated iron roof and a locked door. The building sits at the edge of the Khe Sanh runway and the red sign with yellow lettering sitting inside the barb wire at the building states simply: "Graves Registration— Restricted Area".

Mike graduated from Sylvan Hills High School in North Little Rock in 1964. His father, now Reverend Crowley went to Conway to take over as pastor at the Church of Christ at Robeson & Center soon after. His three youngest sisters will be back in school there in the fall. Debbie Louise is a senior in High School. Candice Gwenn, a junior in Junior High School, and Marsha Layne is a ninth grade student. Another sister, Mrs. Sammie Lynn Lacey, and a brother, Ed M. Crowley, Jr., are still in North Little Rock. Mike's wife is the former Judy Ann Lynch, daughter of Mr. and Mrs. Lloyd R. Lynch of North Little Rock. Mike's mother and father live in Conway.

"We made three amphibious landings on our way over," says Mike "and then we landed here in September of 1966. Gee, that seems like a long time ago."

Mike's first eight months in Vietnam were spent as a forward observer with a "line company". His job was to be at the very front of the action, determine where enemy lines began and his own lines ended. Then Mike would decide where he wanted the bombs and artillery to hit, and have his radio operator send that information back to the fire control center in the rear. During those months "we did a lot of walking", says Mike. In the Marines, the infantryman is called a "grunt". And Mike readily admits that "The FO is just a 'grunt', even if the Corps does say we are artillerymen."

The twenty-year-old Sergeant did a lot of patrolling then and had some raw experiences from his first day out. "We were at 'Three Gates to Hell' that day", Mike recalled. "It was a small village that the Vietcong had really fortified. It was surrounded by barb wire, punji sticks, and machinegun bunkers so that the only way in was through these three gates about a hundred yards apart. The instant we got through the first gate they cut us down with automatic weapons fire. We tried to bring some tanks down to blast through, but the second gate had a big tank trap in front of it so that ended that idea."

Probably the worst thing about his old job was the sniper fire. "I had to move up and down the lines a lot to see what was happening and where everyone was. Of course the snipers would spot me immediately and start sighting in on me. But I just had to sweat the first round. If the guy missed with that, we'd spot him and blow him out. Then I only had to worry about the next first shot from the next sniper."

But there were a lot of bad experiences for Mike and he "sorta got used to them". One particularly hard fight at Hill 55 was nicknamed 'Dodge City'. His description: "Oh, it was gunsmoke, shoot 'em up, bang bang . . . you know."

Some things seemed funny to him—after they were over. There was a guy they called "Rock" in his old platoon. "We named him after the song 'Rock Feels No Pain'. He never got the least upset no matter how rough it was."

"Then there was the time we were in our foxhole laying on some banana leaves we had put down to keep us out of the mud. The tips of the leaves stuck up over the edge of the hole and when the fire started the machinegun bullets were hitting the ends of the leaves. We could hear them hitting up there. The radio was outside the hole and we had to get it; but I sure didn't want to stick my head up for it. So the Corporal and I had a little discussion over "Marine Corps discipline" to see who would get it. The radio I mean. It took about five minutes but Marine Corps discipline finally won out", says the Sergeant.

The tension in the field was always high for Mike. Once, the Vietcong tossed two grenades at his hole from only a few yards away. One exploded just outside the hole, but the one that came inside "right between my legs", was a 'dud'. "Many times like that, and like the time I had the collar shot off my flak jacket, and they'll turn your shirt around backwards and lace you up and carry you off laughing."

As his tour of duty drew near an end Mike missed "the everyday sounds of home, the life and hubbub, and the relaxation." He likes to coon hunt and plans on going out with his father's blue tick hound, Ace, when he gets back home. Ace was a gift to his father from Mike. "And I bought my wife, Judy, a new Volkswagon. It only costs me about seven dollars a month to live over here."

After he gets out of the Marines Mike wants to go back to his old work as an electrician. While he was in school and before he went on active duty he used to work for Healey Brothers Electric Company (of Conway and North Little Rock) and is anxious to start working at his trade again.

"But that will have to wait until I have time to buy a big twenty-five cent chocolate malt", grins Sgt. Crowley.

Thirty-four year old Frank Lambert is a man who is "getting short"; after 12 months in Vietnam, he will leave here in September and after 17 years in the Marine Corps he will retire in 3 more years. The thirty-four year old first lieutenant looks over the burned hills outside his office on the outskirts of DaNang and says simply, "I'm too old to be over here by myself." He would much prefer to be back home in Conway with his wife, the former Jane Shepherd, and their four children.

Presently, Frank is the adjutant for the Third Amphibious Tractor Battalion, First Marine Division. As adjutant, he is the chief administrative officer for some 800 men who spend their days roaming the hills around DaNang in search of the enemy. All the paper work that goes along with a combat operation is Frank's responsibility. That work includes complete reports on all casualties, at least on a day in the Third Amtracs, all awards (medals), promotions, legal matters, and reports on supplies needed. Much of the work is essential to the continued good morale of the men. For example, Frank sees to it that a man from his battalion who is wounded and sent out to the hospital ship, "Sanctuary", has his mail follow him there, otherwise, the wounded marine is faced with the prospect of laying wounded in a hospital with all his mail stacked up seventy miles away.

Then there are the little things. Lt. Lambert received a call from an air control officer who wanted to know why a man from Third Amtracs had failed to show up for his flight out of Vietnam the previous week. Frank set the machinery in motion to find out why. "Can you imagine anyone who has a chance to get out of this hole missing his flight?", Frank asks ironically.

"The whole thing has been unpleasant" for him. Sitting at his desk he says "nothing unusual has happened to him there".

39

Of course, in Vietnam the 'usual' is frequent mortar attacks and regular violent deaths. Lambert's desk is haphazardly decorated. Pictures of his children; three small flags, the United States, Arkansas, and the Marine Corps; a large glass jar of Aunt Mahalias Old Fashioned Stick candy; yellow flowers; a guitar with one string missing; and a small black decal with a white center labeled "panic button". And then, of course, there's the thick sheaf of casualty reports.

Most of the causalties in Lt. Lambert's battalion are caused when the amtracs hit mines. "Until Vietnam", says Lambert, "the amtrac was used only "ship to shore" as a method for Marines to be placed on the beach to attack. We are using them in Vietnam now as a land vehicle with the regular tank-infantry type maneuvers. The amtracs move in first to detonate mines and provide a shield, and the troopers follow along behind."

One particularly effective innovation for the amtrac has been developed using the LVT E1 engineer's amtrac. With its long aluminum teeth scraping a pathway, the fourteen ton behemoth, fires a rocket with a "string", which is actually electric detonating cord; attached to the "string" are about a dozen ten pound blocks of c-4 plastic explosive. By detonating these blocks a safe pathway may be cleared through jungle, barb wire, and mines, and simultaneously, a good many tunnels, favorite VC hiding places, may be discovered.

Frank believes most of the really big military pushes by the Vietcong and North Vietnamese are over now. "We've just about wound up the fighting. Now we have to win the people." But already he's seen progress in that direction. A few months ago the Vietcong used to probe the perimeter of the Third Batallion through a small village within sight of Frank's office. "We started giving them scrap building materials and some food for their animals, and some medical care. And now, whenever Charlie tries to make a move through the Village, the people let us know in advance. A few weeks ago, one of the village elders brought us a grenade the VC had left in the village. We offer a big reward for any weapons brought in; we tried to give him $500 but he wouldn't take it. Just smiled."

Frank is also the "industrial relations man" for the battalion. From time to time he goes around to nearby villages and hires carpenters, mess (cafeteria) workers, secretaries, and laborers to do odd jobs around the compound. The people he hires are getting better pay than they have ever had; the highest wage is equivalent to about 25 cents an hour; the lowest, 12 cents an hour.

During his seventeen years with the Marine Corps, Frank has served all over Asia and the Caribbean. He started out as a machine gunner back in 1950. He met his wife, Jane, in Little Rock while he was on recruiting duty in Little Rock from 1951 through 1956. Then in 1960 he was chosen to be one of the first candidates in the Marine Corps' newly established Warrant Officer program. On successful completion of that, he was commissioned and sent to Headquarters Marine Corps in Washington, D. C. While he was there he was in and out of the White House, the Pentagon, and the Capitol as often as his wife was in and out of the local grocery store.

His job there, as a courier of classified information, was the most demanding of all his duties. "I'd work all day, then when I'd get home, the kids would want to go on a picnic down to Manassas or Bull Run." He gleefully recalls the day a repairman came to do some work at their house trailer in Virginia. "He saw my Arkansas Traveler certificate hanging on the wall, and turned around to my wife and said 'Say, is your husband an Ambassador?' ".

Lt. Lambert has started playing the guitar since he arrived in Vietnam. He hasn't learned too many tunes yet, but is partial to country and western music. He especially wanted to thank Jimmy Higgins and Marv Jenkins at Radio Station KBEE in Conway for sending two full tapes of country and western music to him. Since he received it, it has been played in the mess hall and is now in the battalion music library.

After he retires in 1970, Frank is anxious to get back to Conway. "I live just a block from Hendrix, and right across the street from Coach (Ivan) Grove. My wife's parents run the Sands Motel, there, and I just want to get back and spend time with my friends and family. I really miss the kids running around under foot. Of course, I have the troopers running around under foot to take their place; and I scream at them too . . . but it's not the same."

Frank plans on going to college at Hendrix after retirement and would then like to look into trying the ministry in the Church of Christ.

Right now, Lt. Lambert is waiting. He laughs about the picture of himself with a mustache that he sent to his wife. "She showed it to my kids and asked if they noticed anything different", says Lambert. Susan, three, whispered, "ooooh, does it hurt?" Allen, 12, exclaimed "Cool man!" John, 8, and Scott, 7, ignored the mustache, calmly examined the photo and inquired, "What's he doing wearing the pistol under his arm instead of on his hip where it is supposed to be?"

Da Nang, July 11

"The Vietcong would run out of this 'friendly village' and this big pretty pagoda that was right in front of our position;

41

they would open up on us with everything they had and then run back into the village as we started firing back. We aren't supposed to shoot into friendly villages but Charlie had hit us out of that village about three times; so the Lieutenant got mad and we blasted the village. I was plenty glad; the bullets had been tearing into the sandbags I had been hiding behind. After the artillery got through with the place we moved in. Most of the dead had been dragged away, but there was a lot of blood around. Since then, the friendly villagers only stay in the 'vill' during the day. At night they leave."

With these words, L/cpl. Otis L. Phillips of Searcy, described his worst experience while he was in Vietnam. He hopes he won't have any more. "I haven't seen too much action here in Vietnam—but what I've seen, man, it wasn't nice."

This is Phillip's second tour with the United States armed forces . . . and it will be his last. He's been in Vietnam since last January and when he leaves here in 4 months, he's looking forward to getting back to Arkansas. Talking with a fellow Arkansan about home the names of Augusta, Bald Knob, Bradford, were mentioned. "It sure feels good to hear those names," says Phillips.

The 26 year old Marine, who was raised by his grandmother, Narcissa Horton, and his uncle, Nornelle Horton, spent one tour of duty with the Army after he graduated from White County Training School in 1959. With his military obligation out of the way he headed back home, and started working for International Shoe Company and Birds Eye Division frozen foods in Searcy; but the pay was low, his hours were long, and in April of 1965 he married a girl he had grown up with: Alma Turner, daughter of Mrs. Violet Turner of Searcy. With family responsibilities, he decided to spend three more years on active duty "to get squared away" before he went back home for good to try and start his own little business, or maybe work at Remington Rand. Otis decided to join the Marines "just because I had heard so much about them; I wanted to see how it would be."

The Marines haven't been bad for him. A Lance Corporal now, he's just been selected to attend non-commissioned officers training in DaNang. He's worked with some form of artillery during all his time in the service. Before he started NCO training, his specialty was the 106 millimeter recoilless rifle, a near 500 pound "rocket gun" that has a range of almost five miles. After he finishes his NCO training, he will go back to his company and with his new rank of corporal, take command of all maintenance work on the artillery weapons in his company.

While he talked of Searcy and the friends he had there ("Be sure and say hello to George Hendrix for me") he cooly sighted his Marine compass on some distant hills, made quick calculations on some maps piled on a sandbag bunker, then picked up his radio and told them the target on which he wanted the artillery to fire. "It's sorta like back when I was working on one of the merit badges for my Eagle scout when I used to go to Camp Quapaw", he said.

Otis admits he didn't understand too much about the war before he came over; and he says it's still hard. As he watched his explosions six miles away he explained, "Some of the guys who first get here find it real hard. They don't trust anyone; they think all the Vietnamese are the enemy. But after a while they realize most of these people are as frightened as they are.

"If you try and understand the people and show them you are concerned about them you get real good results," Otis says. "If we can just convince the people we are here to help them, the North Vietnamese won't stand a chance."

"The feeling of power is a little frightening," says "Lightning Bolt 7". "A word from me and a whole mountainside will disappear; a village will be destroyed; perhaps hundreds of men may die. But I like it because I can save a lot of American lives in my job."

"Lightning Bolt 7" is the code name for Mike Fairhead of Jonesboro—a forward observer for the artillery that supports and protects the men of the First Air Cavalry Division operating in the rugged central highlands of South Vietnam. The red-haired, blue eyed First Lieutenant, son of Mr. and Mrs. J. M. Fairhead of Jonesboro, has been in Vietnam for six months. He volunteered to come to Vietnam immediately after he graduated in 1966 from the University of Arkansas where he was cadet battalion commander of his ROTC unit. "I figured I'd be here sooner or later and thought I might as well get it over with," Mike explains. "Besides, I wanted to see what it was like . . . and it was a good chance to get assigned to the First Air Cavalry; I guess I wanted to check them both out."

Mike feels that he had good training before he came here. He spent three weeks in Panama in jungle training. "It was rough," he laughs, "but for an old country boy like me never out of the States before, it was fascinating." But after all the really dense jungle there, Mike really hasn't been in an area where he can use what he learned. Vietnam's central highlands regions are composed of incredibly steep and heavily wooded hills. "But not real jungle like Panama," says Mike.

He arrived in Vietnam during Tet, the Vietnamese New Year that is celebrated by a temporary pause in the daily slaughter. He had been here four days, when a battle began ending the truce. "It was near Hill 26," Mike recalls. "A patrol had made contact with an unknown size enemy force. I was in

44

the battalion 'reaction force' that 'mounts up' and roars into any battles in our area. "There had not been time for artillery to 'prep' . . . that is pound out . . . the area where Mike was headed. He was in Chopper Number Six and as he landed they began to receive heavy enemy fire from three sides. Within two hours six men were dead and eight wounded. Artillery was the only thing that could keep them alive during the night. Mike was with only thirty men and they were trapped in a perimeter only 100 yards across. "We found out later that we had landed right in the middle of the 18th North Vietnamese Army Regimental Headquarters." said Mike. "But that night I was really scared. Every time anyone moved or exposed themselves all hell would break loose. I just lay on the ground and stuck my head as far in the dirt as I could. I prayed more that night than I had in my whole life."

There was another FO still with the company, so in that first fight, Mike was assigned to move out to the edge of the perimeter with a machinegun and take on any attack that might start during the night. "The artillery put 4000 shells around us for protection during the night. But right after it let up I saw this VC crawl out of a hole and start walking around with a candle! I couldn't believe it! I guess he thought we had gone. Well, we didn't want to hit him with the machinegun and expose our position, so we let him get pretty close and then grenaded him. I still can't figure out what the hell he was doing with a candle out there."

The next day as American troops moved through the battle area, Mike got his first look at what the artillery he would soon be directing can do to a man. "We found a lot of bodies around. This was all brand new to me. They were blown all to pieces . . . all messed up. We even found two snipers tied up in some palm trees. They had been giving us most of our casualties. We couldn't see them. But that artillery just had to come close with an aerial burst and it was goodbye Charlie."

After watching friends die on that last day of Tet, and particularly on his next operation, when Mike saw "friendly village" after "friendly village" suddenly spew bullets at his company, and realized that a lot of the fire came from women in the villages, Mike began to take some offense at the "rules of engagement" that govern all United States Military activity. The rules of engagement state that no American unit can open fire until fired upon. This is particularly carefully enforced when working in a mountain area where inaccurate maps or an overeager FO can destroy a whole village that really is friendly. Mike and other FO's have developed their own technique for this situation.

45

"Usually I'll have a smoke round fired into the village first," says Mike. It's harmless . . . just makes a big pop and puts a long comma of smoke over the village. The people know what it means too. It's sort of an omen to them now. They realize we have them zeroed in and that if they open fire on us we can wipe them out."

The FO has a tremendous responsibility. Perhaps that's why only officers, like Mike, are allowed to call in the massive power of American artillery. The FO is the eyes and ears for the artillery. When Mike looks at a map and calls forward those shrieking shells he does so with the knowledge that his maps are inaccurate, that the jungle around him obscures his vision, and that his own troops may be hit by the shells, "Sometimes I can only hear the explosions and have to correct by sound." But he cannot hesitate.

"It's no good if the rounds are far away when I call them," says Mike, "it's got to be close. That's what the troops want and what I want. When the shells start coming in we put on our 'pots' (helmets), get in a hole and let the shrapnel sing over our heads. We know if its that close the enemy can't get in on us.

"But I have to be careful. It's horrible to kill one of our own men. And when I'm calling for an airstrike the risk is even greater. The pilots are upstairs and I'm downstairs and things don't look the same to us. A tree from below doesn't look much like a tree from above. Usually I'll have the artillery put a colored smoke round where I want the planes to hit; or I'll use a grenade rifle to shoot some smoke out so the planes can see what I'm after. Then, I make sure he knows where we are. We never have a plane make its bomb run directly over our heads . . . we have it cross in front of us. That way if he misses a little the bomb goes off to our right or left. But if he is flying over us and the bomb falls short, then trouble. But I won't even ask for the planes to use their machine guns on a target near me. Those things are as erratic as fleas on a dog."

Mike has artillery at his disposal that can "mail" him a shell from as far as twenty miles away. Not only does he tell the artillery where to fire but also what kind of shells to use. He has a wide selection. White phospherous rounds explode a dense chemical that burns everything around and can be extinguished only by cutting off all air from it. By requesting a variable time fuze he can have the shell explode twenty feet above ground so it will blast down into holes and trees. He can use smoke rounds to cover troops movements. Or he can call forth the usual high explosive rounds that kill everything above ground within a thirty yard radius and kills most things within a seventy yard radius.

46

If the enemy is in an underground bunker, he will call in a shell from one of the eight inch guns. These monsters weigh 200 pounds and will bury themselves deep in the ground before exploding and caving in the bunkers.

A typical call by Lt. Fairhead will sound like this: "Royal Purple this is Lightning Bolt 7". "Go ahead Lightning Bolt 7". "Fire Mission Grid 945732. Sniper fire from treeline and bunkers. First round smoke. Direction to follow first round."

After the smoke round lands, Mike will correct the aim. Right 50 meters. Up 15 meters. Repeat with WP and HE.

The standard operation in this war is to call in artillery fire as soon as contact is made with the enemy. This technique has received some criticism, because it gives the enemy time to slip away before U.S. ground troops move on into the area. This procedure is also responsible for a good bit of the high cost of the war in Vietnam . . . estimated at $800 a minute or $500,000 per enemy soldier killed. But Mike has a different view. "Why lose a lot of Americans by trying to push through an area on the ground before softening it up? Sure it costs more and a lot of times the VC get away. But it saves a lot of American lives . . . and when its a question of men or money the United States, unlike the others, prefers to spend a lot of money instead of a lot of lives."

Peace demonstrators at home don't disturb Mike usually. "Sometimes I think about it. We're here fighting and they're home demonstrating. But who's to say what's right? I guess that's part of what I'm fighting for. And I'm proud of it. But sometimes it's a little hard to keep that perspective from day to day."

Mike hopes to get home on "Operation Santa Claus", designed to get men back to the States for Christmas, to be with his mother and father, his brother John 21, a sister Mrs. David W. Sharp, and his thirteen-year old twin sisters Mary Lee and Rosemary. There is also a University of Arkansas senior he's looking forward to seeing. A message for her: "the Pooh says 'hi'."

The soldier's strong husky body is burned brown by the war sun. PFC Jimmy Lee Kettner of Springdale sits in the two inch deep dust of Landing Zone Ollie. He looks out across his squat black howitzers to the palm trees and green mountains beyond and notes glumly, "The worst thing about being in Vietnam is just being here. I've got just, he looks at his calendar watch and pauses, "140 days to go. Last Christmas I had just flown into An Khe. This year I'll be home with my wife, Virginia."

Born in Prairie Grove, the 22 year old Kettner is now with A Battery 77th Artillery supporting the 1st Air Cavalry Division. "Our battery has been lucky," he says. "We've never been hit. Once in April the 18th NVA regiment tried to get us . . . but the choppers pulled us out." Jimmy's battery has only 150 men in it, and is guarded by one company of infantry. The battery bounces from landing zone to landing zone. The LZs, as they are known, have been endowed with such exotic names as LZ Snake, Crystal, Two Bits, Uplift. In former days army units were stationed in forts. But here, artillery as well as infantry ride out after the 'Indians' from helicopter landing zones.

But the names are all that is exotic about these dust holes. "We don't stay in one place for more than three weeks, so we're always sleeping on the ground, or in a hole, or maybe we'll have time to set up some sort of little platform to sleep on. But a good place to sleep has to wait until we build some sort of little bunker with a roof on it to protect us from mortar attacks."

From the air, these pitiful looking, but powerful little islands appear as four hundred yard wide circles with a few strands of barbed wire and some trenches surrounding the deadly efficient guns and men inside. In another war, the artillery would be in a relatively straight line pointed towards

48

the enemy position. But in Vietnam, the enemy position is everywhere and nowhere . . . so the guns are positioned in circles. A new mounting has been developed for the howitzers to allow them to be turned 360 degrees in a matter of seconds.

Outside the configurations of the weapons, things are pretty much the same as before. "Up until about three months ago, we were still using World War II ammo—the dates, 1943, 1944, were still on them. We're almost through the Korean stock now and getting in some new stuff. But it seems to me like it's, tune in again next week, same guns, same ammo, same way, different place!"

The hours of work are erratic. Some days will be twenty four hours on the job. Others will be slow. When the guns aren't firing, new ammo must be fused. Jimmy had screwed the five pound fuses on to 460 rounds of ammo that day. At seventeen turns per shell that was 7,820 twists. "We unload the truck, stack the shells, fuse the shells, put them on the "mule" to take them over to the gun, and then restack them. Every five thousand rounds the howitzer requires a new barrel. How many times a year are they changed? "Well, pretty often," laughs the blonde-haired Kettner. "We've fired way over a million rounds since the start of the year. We fired 1200 rounds yesterday . . . we killed one VC and found one weapon."

In addition to the heat and dirt, the men of A battery have to endure the constant noise of the guns. A million explosions every six months makes a lot of violent sounds. "The first day I was opening some ammo near the front of the barrel. I didn't get my hands over my ears in time and the blast deafened me. My ears are really bad now. I have to look at my watch to see if its running. I can't hear it tick when I put it up to my ear. We have to shout at some of the guys just to get them to hear us at all."

While scratching the ears of the battery mascot, a small brown and black striped dog named "Tiger" ("he's been on more chopper rides than most of the guys over here") and listening to the sounds of an Elvis Presley record drifting from an adjoining 'hootch', Jimmy talked of his job. "We worry about hitting our own men and whether we're doing a good job to support the guys out there. We really worry about hitting our guys. B battery hit one of our helicopters the other day. The guns are great for burning down a village . . . we can hit one nine miles away."

Back in Springdale, Jimmy worked at Lee Gibson's Skelly Station. He likes to mess around with cars but since being in Vietnam the only thing he's had a chance to drive has been the "mule" . . . a powerful springless little cargo carrier used to cart the 60 pound shells from the ammo dump to the guns. When he gets out of the army PFC Kettner wants to use the GI bill to study mechanics for awhile, and then hopes to open his own service station.

Another Arkansas boy, PFC Jimmy Lee Cook, of Blytheville, works with Jimmy. The two of them have the secondary job of harassing six Texans in their battery about how bad the Razorbacks are going to beat the Longhorns come next fall. "We really bug 'em" says Kettner. "It gives us something to kid around about. We make a point of not worrying. If you start worrying about things it just makes it harder on you."

A mass of dust jumped into the air and bit at him as a helicopter landed nearby. "Boy I'll be glad to get out of here and get back to the icebox, and TV, and clean clothes . . . life's so easy back home."

Jimmy is the son of Mr. and Mrs. Bill Kettner of Springdale. His brother Donald Ray, 16, is a student at Springdale High School. His wife, Virginia is the daughter of Mr. and Mrs. Eulis Smith of Springdale.

Even when the booby traps started exploding, there was no real show of excitement among the men in Corporal David Scott's patrol. The heat, the pain, the misery, the casualties and the long walk back were all part of a way of life that has enveloped Scott and will hold him prisoner until he leaves Vietnam . . . in mid-September. This is his two-day biography.

First Day   1200 hours:

'Scotty', the son of Mr. and Mrs. Robert Scott of West Memphis, got the word on the patrol at noon when he went down to unload a truck of sand. As he and a buddy surveyed the work in front of them, some of the trucks crew were talking: "Hey, what we need all this sand for, anyway?", asked a sweating young Negro.

A Marine with torn trousers and a filthy tee shirt looked at him coldly, "To bury you with, man."

Scotty began shoveling out the sand and soon found himself working alone as his buddy slipped away to sleep. He returned to his squad hootch in time to have some c-rations before he threw on his gear to go out on a night listening post (LP).

1800 hrs: Stirring a tin of cheddar cheese into his c-ration ("turkey, boned") Scotty talked to the reporter. He has been in this country since last August. During his thirteen month tour he has been working the same thirty square mile area. He's seen no change in it since he arrived. A loud argument behind him is halted as the platoon sergeant yells, "Hey, keep it down, there's a man trying to get some information from Scotty; he's a reporter."

"A reporter? Is that right?" he laughs. Scotty turns around and smiles hugely, "Yeh, I'm an important man." The whole squad starts laughing and rolling around.

51

"Hey" another Marine yells . . . "That Johnson, he keeps talking about how good the war is going over here—send that fucker thirteen months of ham and lima beans 'c' rations and then let him tell us that."

Scotty downed a mouthfull of warm, reconstituted milk from the Foremost plant in Danang. Face puckered in disbelief that anything could taste so bad, he says, "I've seen a lot of guys get killed over here, and go home with no legs and all shot up. And then we go into a 'vill' and ask these people where the VC are and all we get is 'con biet', I don't understand! Shit! They understand!"

"Hey, tell him about that guy with crutches."

"Yeah, we were out in a free fire area, that is, anybody that we see there is considered to be a bad guy. This young fellow, about twenty or so, came diddily bobbin' down this rice paddy dike with a hoe over one shoulder and a pair of crutches over the other. He saw us about the same time we yelled at him. He threw the hoe away and started trying to get up on his crutches and smile. We didn't even believe that! We didn't even let him try and explain that. We must have put forty rounds in him."

"My girl, Glenda, up at ASU wrote me the other day and says she's going to be afraid of me when I get home. Can you believe that?"

"You should have seen old Scotty a few weeks ago. He'd scratched his hands all up on Union II, and there was puss all over them . . . that's the way this damn place is . . . and the flies were all around him. He'd go to sleep at night and his hands would be black with all the flies. During the day he'd walk around with his hands out in front of him like, like one of those what do you call them? Yeh, praying mantis . . . and the flys all over."

"That Union II was a rough operation," said Scotty. Fourteen days without contact. Fourteen days! We'd go up and down those hills and the vines and crud were so thick we had to hack our way for every step. And there were bugs and gnats and those flys and it was hotter than I've ever been. Sometimes we'd go for a couple of hours in one direction up a hill and then it would get too thick and we'd have to back down and try another way up. We were screaming and cussing we were so mad and frustrated. Cisco over there is always kiddin' and joking, but you guys remember when he just sat down and said 'God help us'. And he was serious."

Scotty pulled out a photo of a former squad member who was wounded and sent home. "Look at this." The photo showed a Vietnam veteran in his glory. Sitting by a swimming pool with a beer in his hand, a grin all over his face, and a girl sitting on each knee. "Oh it's gonna be so nice to get back!"

Scotty, a '64 graduate of West Memphis high school, who attended the University of Arkansas and Arkansas State University before joining the Marines has ordered a red 442 with a black vinyl top and plans on driving ("I'll never walk again the rest of my life") and relaxing for a couple of months before he goes back to ASU to complete college.

2030 hours: "Give me a man. We need some work done up here!" The voice drifted down the darkened pathway to the first squad hootch. Cisco mocked it, "Give me a man, give me a man. Hell, the Marine Corps ain't nothing but a bunch of faggots always yelling 'give me a man'!"

The Sergeant sent Cisco out on the work detail and Scotty began putting on his gear to go out on a listening post. The squads alternate all duties. The LP is one of the least popular. It consists of three men moving about four hundred yards outside the camp perimeter at night and keeping watch for any enemy advance on the camp. If VC are spotted the LP's duty is to open fire immediately, regardless of how many are there, and simultaneously to radio back into the camp. Scotty had the duty from 2100 until 0100.

2200 hours: The four man LP was assigned to move down the main road outside the camp and then set up in a field off to one side. But a quickly whispered conversation and even quicker glance at the wet muddy field produced an immediate agreement to stay on the road.

Splitting into teams, they sat on either side of the road facing outwards. One man in each team stretched out to sleep. An hour on, and an hour off was the program. Scotty took first watch and spent ten minutes dousing himself with the pungent mosquito repellant he carried. His M-16 had a bullet in the chamber and the safety was off. He did not expect contact that night but he was ready just in case. A full moon was rising and would soon cast so much light over the field that the LP would be clearly visible. Hopefully, anyone who might spot the LP should also be visible.

The first two hours were uneventful. Then, someone back in camp, forgetting the location of the LP, became nervous and fired three flares immeditely over Scotty's head. There was nothing the four could do but lay flat on their backs, hope no VC were around, and curse the moron who had fired the flares. The radioman, calm, considering the circumstances, called in and reminded the camp he was out there. Then all was quiet again. The mosquitos continued biting. Scotty threw on more repellant; wiped away the night sweat and went back to waiting.

Second day 0130: Back in camp Scotty discovered the new Lieutenant had taken some of the other members of his squad out on a "scorpion": a night ambush. With the squad thus reduced he would have to stand guard duty along with everyone else who had just returned from the LP. They muttered and cursed the new Lieutenant who had just arrived in Vietnam two weeks before. Then Scotty moved out to his guard position. Sitting on the sandbags, he laid three grenades out in front of him, checked the detonators for the claymore mines and thought about how tired he would be at dawn when the patrol started.

0630: "Rise and shine", some fool cheerfully yelled into the sleeping first squad.

"Rise and shine," screamed an outraged squad member. "Where is that asshole!" Quickly Scotty began putting on his boots. "Hell, I haven't even had time to brush my teeth" moaned the squad machinegunner, Clennan.

"Brush your teeth!" said Cisco incredulously. "I haven't even had time to get mine dirty."

The Marines began forming for the patrol, complaining as they discovered the new Lieutenant was changing their assignments. "Every new officer has some new way to do things," said Scotty: "There's no use griping. We just do it." The stench from the combined sweat and mosquito repellant on the men was overpowering. "It's worse than the locker room of our football team," said the former Blue Devil halfback.

The patrol started moving, Scotty in position, seven men back from the "point" of the patrol. "Usually, I'm number three he said. But the Lieutenant's got everything all screwed up."

Passing through the camp gate the patrol of eighteen men headed toward their first checkpoint, a destroyed bridge that crossed a good sized stream. The men would have to wade the stream so they tossed several grenades into it first in hopes of destroying any booby traps the VC may have placed during the night. They were casual about it. Tossing them in then turning their backs and strolling away with their hands over their ears. The explosions sent umbrellas of water into the air. And then Scotty started across. Dripping water he moved on across a road and into some banana fields.

The area of the mudflats is a free fire zone. Once heavily populated, it is now used as a supply and staging area by the Vietcong. There are quite a few houses in the area, but they are all burned and gutted, with walls and ceilings missing. The delicate pastel colors of the walls and the fragile tiled roofs and floors are bullet scarred. Inside some of the houses a chipped rice bowl will lay on the floor where it has been since its owners left years ago. But occasionally, the rice bowls will have fresh rice in them, and the coals in an old fireplace will still be warm . . . sure signs that Charlie has been there recently.

The patrolling in this area is designed to end its use as a travel route by the Vietcong. The patrols have to cover the entire 12 mile square area but not do it in any systematic way.

Virtually every patrol is watched and plotted by the VC. The moment any pattern develops, they will lay an ambush. As the Delta company commanding officer said, "Our tactics are erratic and unplanned, but our strategy must be systematic."

The patrol that morning had twelve checkpoints, designed to take it across a seven mile area in a five hour sweep. The sixth checkpoint was at the edge of a railway track. Long abandoned, the track was once of great service. In most areas of the country this track could be restored with little effort. It was well built to start with, using steel rather than wooden cross ties. But the VC have ripped the rails loose and, like Sherman, bent them pretzel shaped around trees. Or, sometimes sticking one end in the ground, they have left the rail lengths protruding from the railbed like deformed diving boards that bounce and groan in the wind. Delta company believes the whole length of track will have to be destroyed at some time because it is honeycombed with Vietcong tunnels and weapons caches. And anyway, as Scotty says, "The people won't be able to come into this area for fifty years after the war because of all the booby traps."

It was the booby traps that ended this patrol. Resting below the eight foot high railbed, the Lieutenant sent Scotty and five other men to the top of the bed to keep a watch for an attempted ambush and to see if any VC could be spotted in the area. The men were reluctant to move onto the tracks knowing that it was covered with booby traps. "Hell, this ain't no place for me with only 48 days to go," said Scotty. But he knows he'll be doing this same thing everyday until seven days before he leaves Vietnam. At that time he will be allowed to leave the field and relax for a few days before he gets to return home.

Scotty picked his way carefully up the rusted tracks, found a place in the shade, removed his flak jacket and helmet and rested. His canteens were still full. "I've had water from the rice paddies before without getting sick. But I didn't like it. In fact, the first time I had gook water there was a tadpole in it."

From the top of the tracks the machinegunner twenty yards away had a clear view of a field some four hundred yards across. He had just emplaced his machinegun when he whispered urgently back to the Lieutenant. "Hey, there's somebody moving in and out of the trees over there." Two men moved over to him. Then one froze and pointed at the ground near the machinegunners elbow. "Hey man, don't move. There's a booby trap right next to you."

Propped up by two rocks was an m-29 grenade. With the pin removed, the grenade was kept from exploding only by the pressure of the rocks that held it in place. A slight jar is all that is required to explode the grenade.

In quick succession, two more booby traps were spotted along the twenty yard stretch of track where Scotty was stationed. "Well, stay away from them" said the Lieutenant. "And hold your fire. Let's call in some artillery and see if we can drive those people towards our position."

Moving in and out of the trees, and dressed in white pajamas and the ubiquitous straw hat, at least seven people could now be seen.

The artillery shells whistled in over Scotty's head and hit in the tree line where the people were moving. But they started running the other way. Immediately Scotty opened up on them as did the other five men on the tracks. Several of the VC went down. But whether they were hit or just diving for cover was impossible to tell. Another machinegun was brought up and then a loud flat blast sent Scotty and the others to the ground. The lieutenant screamed and fell backwards. Cisco just groaned and grabbed at his leg. The man with the machinegun was laying on his face writhing. Another booby trap had been found.

Altogether five men had been wounded. The lieutenant and the machinegunner had been hurt the worst. One man who was jumping and yelling turned out to be in ectasy . . . not pain. He had a slight wound in the arm. But it was his third wound and that meant he was headed straight home, after only seven months here. He smiled the rest of the day. Scotty felt the old shrapnel wounds in his neck and allowed as how he would just as soon wait out his time. He wanted no more wounds.

The squad leader had been one of the wounded, so now Scotty was the new squad leader. He laughed about it. Then, he helped supervise the making of a stretcher from some canvas and two poles of bamboo. The wounded machinegunner was placed on the stretcher and the long walk back into the camp began. No helicopters were available to medevac the wounded so Scotty would have to help carry the stretcher out to a point where some tanks from camp could reach them.

The walk with the stretchers took about thirty minutes. The tanks had been halted short, unable to move across a graveyard because it had been mined. Immersed in sweat, Scotty finally reached the tanks and loaded the wounded. He started leading the remnants of the patrol, eleven men, back into camp. He reached camp at three o'clock that afternoon, just in time to rest a few hours before he had to go out on a night ambush.

Mike Hester is a Marine. A graduate of the United States Naval Academy class of '65, his crisp uniform, straight back, and bull neck are straight off a recruiting poster. For the last eleven months Mike has been the commanding officer for a platoon of fifty men who have been engaged in almost constant combat, in an area below the DMZ stretching from the South China Sea on the east to the mountainous Vietcong hideouts in the jungles of Laos to the West.

The son of an ex-Marine, Mike arrived in Vietnam in September of 1966 along with the brand new 26th Marine Regiment. "When we started over," Mike says, "all our equipment was brand new . . . and so were all my men." Starting out with 47 privates right out of boot camp, Mike trained his men and then brought them to Vietnam. After one practice assault in the Phillipines, Mike's platoon started operations in an area north of DaNang. Any romantic notions about war ended for Mike right away.

"Those were hard days. There were booby traps everywhere and we kept finding them. During one two month period we took fifty casualties before anyone even shot at us. Losing four or five men a day, I was down to only eighteen men in my whole platoon after a while. One boy in my platoon, from Hope, stepped on a 155 shell. It was horrible—blew off both his legs and an arm. It was so long before we could retaliate." After that it was apparent that new tactics would have to be adopted. And they were.

Mike's platoon, and the others in his company would move into an area, separate, and operate for five to seven days at a time, day and night, in enemy territory. Springing ambush after ambush, morale went up in his platoon and their own casualty figures came down. In contrast with their first efforts

Sgt Gregory Cray of Batesville sits in a turnip patch north of Saigon in the village of Hea Nhut. "Charlie ain't nobody's fool!" (top left)

Staff Sergeant Elmer Taylor of Pocahontas. (top right)

Capt. Don Hatfield of Ft. Smith (left) Ed Bryson of Russellville, at Di Am (bottom)

PFC Birnes Penix of Wilmot: "The night patrols really bug me." (top left).
Bob Higgins of Atkins near Cu Chi: "A man just has to be over here to understand how bad it is." (top right).
Sgt. Clarence James Gray of Little Rock: Vietnam 'Rat Patrol'. (Bottom left).
PFC Earnest L. (Mac) McCain in the Iron Triangle: "That mine should have got us." (bottom right).

"Home" for Mac McCain. (top right).

B Troop moves into the Iron Triangle. (left).

A "track" rests before entering the jungle. (bottom right).

A Vietcong rice cache in the Iron triangle. (top left).

Some of the VC rice come from Arkansas. (top right).

Tommy Thompson of Little Rock, a Marine helicopter gunner: "The Medevacs are the best part of the job." (bottom left).

Thompson's view of the area around Danang. (bottom right).

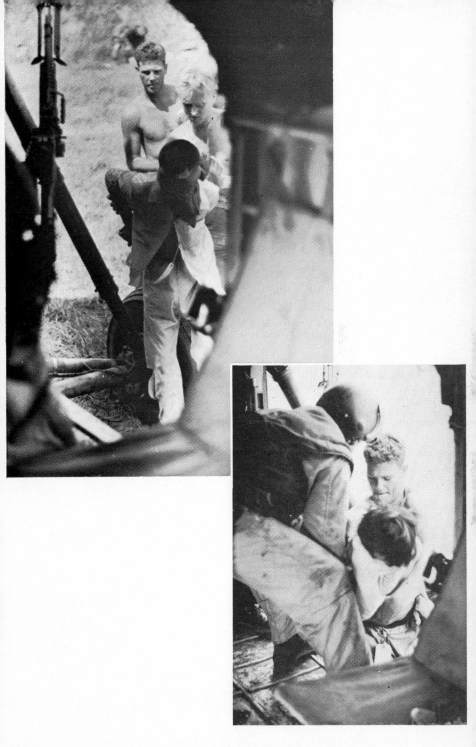

A Vietcong prisoner is hustled towards Thompson's helicopter. (top).

Thompson pulls the prisoner aboard. (bottom).

James Larry Howard of Bright at the DMZ: "The artillery and the motars ... you can hear them coming but you never know whether they will hit you or not." (above).

Lt. Col. Sam Beal of Little Rock and Conway: a fighter pilot in the Corsair; a carrier pilot in World War II; a jet pilot in Korea; now a helicopter pilot in Vietnam. (bottom left).

Floyd E. Bradley of Shirley: "We came out to pick up the bodies." (bottom right).

Billy E. Davis of Pine Bluff: "Those bodies we brought out last night were in pretty bad condition." (top right).

Helicopters resupply Marines along the DMZ at the "McNamara line." (top left).

Tanks pound snipers in the DMZ. (bottom left).

A motar position in the DMZ. (bottom right).

David McLaughlin of Fort Smith: "I like the people; I'm even starting to eat some of their food." (top).

McLaughlin's Arkansas flag flies over his hooch at Phu Bai. (bottom).

Lloyd Parker, Jr. (left) of Melbourne: "I guess the war is good for the Vietnamese who live in Saigon." (top).

Sergeant Michael G. Crowley of North Little Rock and Conway at Khe Sanh. (bottom).

Otis L. Phillips of Searcy: "If we can convince the people we are here to help them
the Vietcong won't stand a chance." (top).

Frank A. Lambert of Conway: "I miss my family. I'm too old to be over here
by myself." (bottom).

like Fairhead of Jonesboro; "The feeling of power is a little frightening." (top left).

William F. Anderson of Searcy: "He just said, 'Oh my God! Oh my God!'; then he died. I couldn't believe it." (top right).

Anderson observes while Fairhead calls in artillery fire: "We're here fighting and they're home demonstrating. But who's to say what's right. I guess that's part of what we're here fighting for." (bottom).

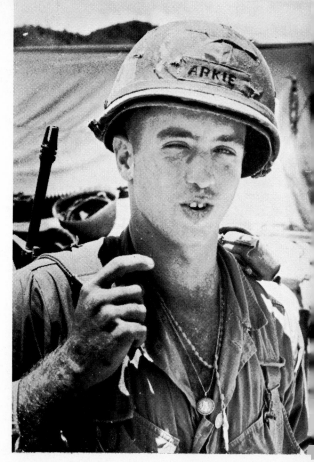

Grane receives the Combat Infantryman's Badge—a brave badge. (top).

Charles J. Grane of Crossett: "The VC tell them we will eat their babies! I'm not kidding!" (bottom).

mmy Lee Kettner of Springdale: "Until three months ago we were still using World War II ammo. We're almost through the Korean stock now." (top left).

st Sgt. Argel Bunch of Dardanelle (left) and Sgt. Major Don Buchanan of Batesville. (bottom).

immy Lee Cook of Blytheville (left) and Kettner: "We worry about hitting our own men and whether we're doing a good job supporting our guys out there." (top right).

David J. Scott of West Memphis, before the booby traps started exploding. (top)
After the booby traps exploded. (middle).
"Oh, it's gonna be so nice to get home." (bottom).

Lt. Mike Hester of Harrison: "I kind of like this flak jacket." 'Bouncing Betties' exploded in front and behind Mike. (top).

Three Arkansans in Danang: Denzil Browning of Crossett (left); Burris Clemons of Thornton (center); Lee Smith of Little Elm. (bottom).

Silver Star Winner
Lt. Bill Wells of Harrison: "The average Vietnamese just wants to be left alone to
farm his land. (top).

Medic Richard L. Coffman of Jonesboro: "We live together, work together, die together."
(bottom).

Fog shrouded Nui Ba Den Mountain (top).

Captain O. P. Williams of Pine Bluff (left) watches his men fire motars onto Black Virgin Mountain: "We'd killed a VC organizer from Hanoi; the mine had torn off the top of her skull..." (bottom).

Burt Renager of West Memphis, (left) a Swift boat skipper: "Welcome to North Vietnam." (top).

Renager on a resupply run below the DMZ: "This is a hell of a way to be spending a nice summer night." (bottom).

The REPOSE at Danang. (top).

Seabee Ty Kelsoe of Greenbrier: "I like building barracks for the troops but we spend an awful lot of time remodeling officer's clubs." (middle).

Orus Puckett of West Memphis aboard the hospital ship REPOSE: "It was an M-26 grenade that got us both." (bottom).

Troy Creamer of Harrison at Ton Son Nhut: "It's just like an assignment in the States." (top).

It sits in the center of Ton Son Nhut: one of the world's most busy airports. (bottom).

David J. Butt of Fayetteville, a Marine sniper: "You either make a mistake and miss or you don't make a mistake and you kill him." (top).

Lester King of Cash, a hospital corpsman lifts a wounded man from a helicopter: "It's awfully sad." (bottom).

Gene Vancleave of Benton. (top).

Commander John Wolfe of Mountain Home. (bottom).

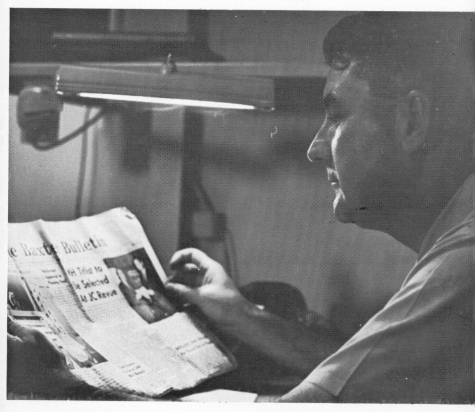

ames Cole of Forrest City, Cannoneer on an M-42 tank. (top).

eorge Zeigler of Malvern. (bottom left).

on Thomas of North Little Rock. (bottom right.

Capt. Edwin T. Gray of Jacksonville feeds 27,000 men each day at Phu Bai. (top left).

Staff Sgt. Cecil A. Garner of Mountain Home by a Marine CH 53A "Sea Stallion" helicopter. (top right).

Lt. Fletcher Moran of Mena(right) and Lt. Eugene William Duderstadt of Gillett (left). (bottom left).

Sgt. Thomas Brimhall of Forrest City at Phu Bai. (bottom right).

the scoreboard for Mike's platoon went to 85 enemy dead to only 1 of his own men killed and five wounded in a period of 30 days.

"We'd hide and wait," said Mike. "On one occasion a 120 man NVA company came through our ambush position. We lay there and watched them. I kept hoping we'd get enough of them together to spring the ambush. But each Vietnamese soldier stayed at least fifty yards from the next one. They were smart. I've been here long enough to respect the NVA soldier for what he is."

The NVA would not always make themselves available for ambush. So Mike tried a newer, and hairier technique. "Our company would send one platoon down a draw, along a creek or something. The hills would rise almost vertically on both sides of us. Over our heads would be the jungle canopy which cut off all sunlight. We were the bait down there, waiting for the NVA to hit us. When they did, we would call in our other companies that would be hiding out waiting. I spent most of my time in the draw."

After eleven months on the line Mike is happy to take over his new job as commanding officer of Sub-Unit Five at Khe Sanh. I can't say I'm too sorry to leave a line platoon. After a year your chances aren't so good. As a matter of fact, a week after he left his platoon for his new assignment his platoon was ambushed and five were killed.

Sub-Unit Five is a general purpose office designed to serve the day-to-day needs of the 3000 plus Marines at Khe Sanh. Mike's varied duties now include watching after a communications section, officer's club, chow hall, motor transport, sick bay, court martials, and providing 25,000 gallons of water a day for the men there.

"Actually Khe Sanh is a pretty quiet place now," says Mike. "But I'll be glad to get away before that monsoon season comes back. Boy! I hated that damn thing!" With a rueful glance at the deepening mud, already over his ankles, Mike trudged the two hundred yards down to the fog-shrouded landing field to watch anxiously for the supply plane that would bring in the food for the camp. "We used to have a little thing called the 'miserable factor'. Ten was the worst possible. During the monsoon we had an awful lot of 9.9 miserable factor."

Although harbingers of the monsoon, in the form of two and three day rains, begin to sweep across the Khe Sanh area in late July and early August, the real agony of those rains doesn't begin until October.

The winds that bring the monsoon normally move up and across Laos from the southwest. The moisture picked up in the Gulf of Siam is dropped in Laos in those months. But as the winds change and sweep from the north across the Gulf of Tonkin, they fill huge layered clouds with water . . . and every drop of that water falls in and around the Khe Sanh area. The soil in the area, all clay with no rocks, turns to a deeper and deeper red brown mud . . . and the mud creeps in and across everything in the camp. Planes slip from the runway, trucks sink into the road bed over their axles, men can sink almost waist deep into the greedy grasping muck.

Feet and hands that are never dry turn soft, tear and peel and then form into huge red sores . . . immersion foot (or hand) it is called. By December the cold is numbing. Rain sweeps in laterally seeming never to strike the ground. Visibility drops to thirty yards. The sun may literally disappear for two months. And at night the camp is so dark it is like trying to walk around with a bag over your head.

An interesting sidelight of life at Khe Sanh is the Bru tribe of Montagnards that live just outside the U.S. fortification. "When the fighting started in this area" comments Mike, "The animals all took off for Laos. Now the Bru have very little to eat. So, it's not surprising to see them come into camp, catch a rat, bash his teeth out with a ball peen hammer, and then after breaking the rat's forelegs, stick the rat in his pocket to take it home to eat."

But, even though the work at Khe Sanh is a good experience for Mike and broadens his background, he still speaks wistfully of his days as a platoon leader. "Once we used the same spot for an ambush four times. That's generally not a very good idea," he says. "We killed four the first time, then twelve, two and finally two more.

Sometimes, trying to set up the ambush could be really frustrating. "Quite often we'd get all scrunched up in the bushes to settle down and wait, and then a bunch of little boys and girls would come over leading their water buffalo and stand there and look at us and giggle. So, what can you do? Up and off again."

Mike has been extraordinarily fortunate during his tour of duty here. He's had a close personal introduction three times to one of the Vietcongs favorite booby traps. Called the "Bouncing Betty", the trap consists of a small mortar shell that, when tripped, leaps several feet into the air and explodes. Mike's flak jacket shows a shredded front and back where the traps exploded just a few feet in front of and behind him. "I kind of like that jacket," he smiles. One of the traps, the third, went up right in front of him . . . but instead of exploding, it just kept going straight up in the air.

The hardest part of the war for Mike has been the way he has to treat his troopers. "It's inhuman the way we have to live here. The men are always filthy and hungry and tired. Yet my job is to keep pushing . . . to make sure they put on clean socks, or buried their garbage, or cleaned their weapons. You can get so tired and discouraged here that it seems like the easiest thing to do is just curl up in the mud and sleep. I can't let them do that and of course they can really hate me for always being on their ass. But it keeps them alive.

Mike misses his good homecooked food at Harrison. "My first 90 days in this country all I had to eat was C-ration, 270 cans of C-ration," he sighs. First thing home, I'll have a big supper, and then wander down to the square and have a coke and just talk with the folks around Harrison. Just talk -and eat." Mike has two sisters, Mrs. Joan Barry of Norman, Okla., and Miss Amy Elizabeth Hester, a senior at Harrison High School.

One of the most common military tactical manuvers in Vietnam is that of "search and destroy" in which American soldiers sweep through a suspected Vietcong area in hopes of finding and then destroying their elusive enemy. With only fourteen days left in Vietnam, 1st Lt. William F. (Bill) Anderson, of Searcy, sat in the deep dust along the Lai Giang River and grinned through his dirt covered face, "I'm concentrating on a strategy of 'search and avoid' right now. "I'm too 'short' to do anymore fighting this time around."

Yet, as a professional soldier, Bill may have to spend several more tours of duty in Vietnam. This is his second time around now. . . and it hasn't been more wonderful than the first. After graduation from Searcy High School in 1956, where Bill was in the Key Club and played in the band, he attended Abilene Christian College for a year, and then enlisted in the Army. By 1962, Bill was in Vietnam working with intelligence at MACV (Military Assistance Command Vietnam). Working out of Saigon, he spent about two weeks of each month in the field. The United State role in Vietnam at that time was supposed to be one of "assistance" and "advice". To Bill the country "appeared to be trying to get a hold of itself." Diem was in power at that time, and Bill occasionally saw the well known Madame Nhu. "I saw her floating around a couple of times. I didn't really have any impression of her other than that she was a mighty attractive lady."

Returning to the United States, Bill was chosen for Officer Candidate School. A little over a year after he received his commission, he had new orders to report back to Vietnam. "I'm fortunate I've got a wife who understands the military," he says. "She realizes I have my orders and my duties to perform". So, leaving behind his wife, Rosemarie, who he met while he was stationed in Germany, and his four children, James, 6, Ralph, 5, Christine, 4, and Jeanette, 1, he stepped back into the holocaust that is Vietnam in July of '66. "It's the same war," he says grimly, "there's just more people on both sides fighting." He didn't volunteer to come over the first time ("Not hardly," he laughs) and he hopes the war will be over before he has to come back again. But Bill, or Andy, as the tall, slender 29 year old is sometimes called, is not a sunshine soldier. Many of his colleagues have left the Army in the face of repeated tours of duty here. But Bill figures that is part of what being a soldier is all about. His medals testify to how fine a soldier he is. The Combat Infantryman's Badge, a Bronze Star for valor, a Bronze Star for meritorious service, an Air Medal for the 80 plus combat helicopter assaults he has been on, the Joint Service Commendation Medal, the Army Commendation Medal, and a Purple Heart.

Spending his final days as commanding officer of B Company 2 bn. 5th inf. 1st Air Cavalry Division, Bill talked easily of his past twelve months here. He started out his tour last year with this same company. "I was with this company for two weeks," he recalls. "On the 17th of August, 1966, the company had been in a big fire fight. The captain and 1st. sgt. had been killed, the executive officer was in the United States on emergency leave, and two platoon leaders had been wounded. Our foxhole strength was about 75%—only about 90 people. The men's morale was down, but when we got them out of the field it didn't take long to bring it back up — clean clothes, shower, mail, a couple days of rest."

A convoy began rolling across the bridge above and behind Bill; a helicopter roared low overhead; some of his men began setting out the hot chow that had been brought in for supper.

In September, Bill became a platoon leader with a Long Range Reconnaisance outfit. The LRRP (pronounced lurp) is not supposed to be a combat unit. It's an intelligence gathering operation. Placed ten to twenty miles from the nearest "friendlies" these small patrols are sent out to watch possible avenues of approach, and to spy on enemy concentrations. It's a hairy job. They must expect to survive on their own for a minimum of five days. "We'd be dropped in by helicopter about a mile and a half from our objective. Then we'd use infiltration procedures to move up closer—that is, folding in the terrain behind us. If we moved a bush to cross a path, we shaped it back up before going further. It's sort of like closing the door behind you.

"Whenever we spotted something we'd report it by radio, then hope like hell the 'something' didn't spot us. If we got in a fight it would take at least 60 minutes to have a helicopter over our area to pick us up. And that's a long, long time if there's a lot of Charlies around."

By November of '66, Bill was a rifle platoon leader with Charlie company 2/5. There were the usual fights, which become monotonous, though certainly not boring. During that time, Bill captured a North Vietnamese Army Lieutenant . . . one of the thousands of NVA soldiers that Hanoi claims are not in the south.

Then, in February of '67 Lt. Anderson's platoon found and destroyed the 8th bn. headquarters of the 18th North Vietnamese regiment. The battalion had been hit hard about six days before and had gone into hiding.

"We found this well shaft. A man had been spotted going in and out of it, so we knew someone was down there. They had dug a tunnel into one side of the shaft about thirty feet down. We had our interpreter yell for them to come out, but that did no good. So we put a man on a rope and lowered him down in front of the cave where he could throw in a tear gas grenade to force them out; they shot him in the stomach as he went down.

"After sixteen hours trying to get them to surrender we said to hell with it and blew them up. We tied a forty pound charge of plastic explosive on a rope, lowered it in front of the cave and exploded it. We were able to bring out five bodies—all killed by the concussion."

"After that we worked day to day on search missions," says Bill. "We would go through a village and take in all draft age young men for interrogation. In some villages we were offered tea; in others, well, the villagers were pretty apprehensive."

After spending his R&R with his wife in Hawaii ("Oh, that was nice. "You couldn't beat it!") Bill became executive officer of Alpha Company 2/5. Alpha's commanding officer was a Captain Lee of Alabama. A graduate of Auburn University, he was a strong, handsome young guy that Bill had been close friends with. "We both had the same rotation date. We were going to be heading home on the same day." Looking over at one of his men lancing a boil on the neck of a fellow soldier, Bill sighed. "On June the twentieth we were on the Nui Mieu Mountain near the South China Sea. A grenade landed right behind Lee. I don't guess he ever knew what happened. After the noise and the black smoke he was lying there on the ground. He just said 'Oh My God! Oh My God!; loud the first time then kind of soft; and then he died. I couldn't believe it."

Now, as c/o of Bravo company, Bill and his men have had a few weeks "rest", guarding the bridge at Bong Son. The area

is relatively safe. And though the hard dust covered grou
pitted with fox holes and bunkers, Bill and most of his
sleep on top of the bunkers or on open ground under
mosquito nets. Keeping clean is difficult due to the dust
is always falling in a fine mist from the convoys on the
by the area. But the warm river offers a fine bath, and
of Bill's men just swim around in it on their rubber air
tresses. Tall palms are scattered everywhere, and their
green contrasts with the brown grass huts they shade. A
the river from the sandbags and foxholes of Lt. Ander
company the burnt orange of the French tiled roofs in Bon
give a dull reflection from the hot sun. Children play all
the river, but stay clear of the deadly claymore mines
protect the rusted steel of the bridge.

Pushing his Razorback crested helmet back from hi
covered glasses, Bill smiles, "I've got a deal with a fellow
Texas. If the Arkansas-Texas game is in Texas this yea
buy the tickets and I'll buy the booze. If the game is in A
sas, vice versa."

All his men had eaten supper so Bill filled his plat
a hot meal and returned to his dining room, a lean-to c
with old rubber ponchos to keep out the rain. The table i
from 105 millimeter howitzer shell boxes, the chairs ar
steel 40 millimeter antiaircraft shell containers. "I don'
miss the TV. But the little things I'm used to are har
without—going out and driving a car; opening the refri
for a cold beer; sitting down to a home cooked meal; re
There's so many things you do at home that you neve
about until you're here—clean clothes, a bath a day, ha

Members of the 1st Air Cav are fortunate in one
With their hundreds of helicopters the men are able
hot meal pretty regularly when they are in a reasonabl
area. That night supper was, turkey, bread, corn, swe
toes, gravy, Kool-aid, and, incredibly, ice cream. "I re
the first time we got ice cream," Anderson laughs. "
way out in the boondocks when a chopper flew over and
for us to cut a landing zone for him. 'Cut an LZ,' he sai
got ice cream for you'. I thought, what the hell is 'ic
the code word for? I didn't realize what they were
about until I saw it—four five gallon cans of ice c
wasn't very good ice cream, but, by God, it was ice cre

It was late evening, and Bill walked the company p
to make sure guards were out and all was well. Two
were playing cards by flashlight, the tanks at the br
the mortars in the camp were firing sporadically to di
any possible enemy approach. A few men carefully
their names with indelible ink on new pairs of jungle

65

Bill checked the company roster with his first sergeant to determine who would be around to receive some awards the next day. A man from each platoon was present to remind them who on the list had been killed or wounded. . . . Lt. Anderson then had a long drink of water from his canteen, lay down on his air mattress, and looked up at his bizarre mosquito net view of the sky over Vietnam. With the warm wind in the palms he went to sleep.

Bong Son, July 14

PFC Charles J. Grano tilted back his head to drain the last few drops of warm water from his green rubber canteen. He tried to ignore the rivulets of sweat making furrows in the thick dust on his face and arms. "It was a beautiful introduction to this place," he says sourly. "Someone told me that we would only average about one fire fight every six months—we had three during my first fourteen days with this company. That gave me a whole new perspective on just about everything, especially on home and education." He looked around him with absolute disgust, "Well, at least we can rest awhile here, now. We need it."

The men in Bravo company, 2 bn 5th Inf 1st Air Cav like Charles Grano. They call him 'Arkie' after his home state and he enjoys the nickname. Arkie's tour of duty in Vietnam began "after I got too smart for everybody." A 1959 graduate of Crossett High School, Grano was in the National Honor Society, and played a clarinet in the band before he went to the University of Arkansas to study business and marketing. He left the University in 1962, the first time he got "too smart", went home to Crossett and worked for a year at Homer Pierce ESSO. The next year he went back to college, this time at Arkansas A and M. Two years there, and he did it again. "I got too smart for everybody one more time . . . and that time I got drafted." He went from Ft. Polk to Ft. Rucker, to Ft. Benning, and then in February of this year his unit was alerted for duty in Vietnam.

He joined Bravo company on June 15th. "We'd been camped up on a mountain when word came in that another company had been pinned down by heavy sniper fire. We jumped on our choppers and they dropped us into the fight. It was funny in a way. I didn't have any thoughts in particular as I jumped off the chopper. The LZ was 'hot', with most of the fire coming from some dirt bunkers built near three hootches on the other side of a rice paddy. Three of us went up to check one of the bunkers after the tanks had hit them pretty good. I was scared to death walking up to it; and I don't mind admit-

who is most likely a Vietcong. Or else, they may just take it down and sell it on the black market."

Arkie's sergeant came by and told him to gather up his gear and fall in. Twenty minutes later standing in the dust and sun, with heat waves rising off the river, the Battalion commander pinned the Combat Infantryman's badge on Charles. The badge, showing two crossed flintlock rifles on a field of blue, is a proud symbol. It testifies that the man who wears it has taken his place in the roles of the long line of American men who have fought faithfully and valiantly in the service of their country. The badge knows no politics. It means only that its bearer has gone through the agony of performing a duty requested by his country and seen as proper by him. It is a brave badge.

Charles is the son of Mr. and Mrs. Charles X. Grano of Crossett. He has three sisters, Mrs. Stella Rous, Letitia, and Sylvia who is a senior at the University of Arkansas. Charles plans on finishing his BA after he leaves the service and then hopes to attend law school at the University in Fayetteville. He asks that a special hello be passed on to Pat and Helen and Sue at the Deluxe in Fayetteville.

"How do I like Vietnam," smiles Sgt. Major Don Buchanan of Batesville. "Well, I fly around a lot in my job, and from upstairs it looks beautiful." Don then laughs and leaves unsaid his more down to earth opinions of his temporary home. The 43 year old career soldier is stationed in the city of Qui Nhon on the coast of Vietnam with the United State's Army 41st Signal Battalion. He spends most of his time in a helicopter with his battalion commander flying two hundred miles out in every direction from Qui Nhon, checking the vital communications network that allows the various American commanders to have some idea of what one another is up to.

Don also keeps an eye on the MARS (Military Amateur Radio Society) facilities in Qui Nhon and in An Khe. Through MARS, American soldiers in Vietnam are able to call home to their families every month. By short wave radio, a ham operator on the West coast is called. He in turn places a telephone call to the soldier's parents, then hooks in the phone to his radio set and poof! 12,000 miles disappear.

In all, Sgt. Major Buchanan is responsible for the communication facilities for two full Divisions of men in this war: the 4th Infantry Division and the 1st Air Cavalry. But the cheerful, highly competent Arkansan is used to it. First entering the Arkansas National Guard in December of 1940, his unit was mobilized and sent to Camp Robinson. He spent those war years in Alaska and then ended up back in North Little Rock in 1945. "I was ready to get out of the Army and make my first million then," says Don, "so I left the Army and went to ASTC in Conway." Three years later Don was back in uniform. Since then he's been in and out of Korea, Germany, Japan and Kentucky, and spent thirty days in the Dominican Republic, a place not noted for especially good communications at any level.

Don looks back fondly on his days at ASTC. "I didn't learn much but I had a darn good time, and I have a lot of friends there." While at Conway, Don played three years of baseball as an outfielder, and spent one year on the football field and basketball court. Studying business and accounting, he was a member of Sigma Tau Gamma fraternity and the 'T' Club. He played football with Dee Brittenum, uncle of Jon, former U. of A. quarterback. He also served with a Sgt. Dickerson at one time who played ball with U. of A. football coach Frank Broyles at Georgia Tech.

Buchanan arrived in Vietnam in April of this year. His working hours are long, and entertainment, needless to say, is pretty limited. Though Don is used to this sort of rigor, many of his men are not. The city of Qui Nhon is off limits to the military after seven o'clock in the evening, and even if it were not, the town has little to offer except ragged, dirty bars selling blackmarket beer or cheap whiskey at exorbitant prices. To keep up his men's morale, Don has helped set up a Soldier of the Month Award. Given monthly to one man in every company the award is phenomenally popular—not so much because of the twenty-five dollar war bond it carries with it but mostly due to the guts of the prize: a three day pass and thirty days off guard duty.

The United States Army has probably set up more orphanages than any other organization in the world. Don's battalion is supplying an orphanage in Qui Nhon that presently has thirty children—and his men are now trying to build a school for the children.

"We don't see too much of the war here", says Don. "But he hopes his nephew, an ASU graduate now in Germany, doesn't have to come to Vietnam. "We have a lot of alerts here in Qui Nhon, but we haven't been attacked yet. I guess my worst problem is trying to build a drainage system that will keep my men out of the water in the monsoons." Then Don nods towards the heavy green hills that overlook Qui Nhon. "Out there on the other side of the hills it's real nasty. It's a war."

Don is married to Mildred McCraw from Auburn, Kentucky. They have two children, Karen 11, and Gary 6. His niece is Mrs. Billy Ball who lives in Searcy. One sister, Clara, works in Senator J. William Fulbright's office in Washington.

Qui Nhon, July 15

"Seventy five days left in Vietnam and two years left in the Army," says 1st Sgt. Argel L. (Bob) Bunch of Dardanelle. "Then I can get back to that big Lake Dardanelle and fish all day long. That's sure gonna be the first thing I do when I get home!" Bob is the 1st Sgt. with Bravo Company of the 41st Sig. Battalion and the Non Commissioned Officer in Charge (NCOIC) of the communications center at Qui Nhon. The lean, sun-tanned Arkansan has been in Vietnam since last October, first as a platoon Sergeant. His biggest job now is to keep all the highly technical communications jobs in his company filled. Every week men are being rotated out of Vietnam and back to the States, so every week Bob has to be sure he has someone on hand who can fill the vacancies as they occur. "Some months I lose ten men . . . other months I'll lose 40," he says.

The communications equipment that is run by his company handles everything from supplies, to casualty reports, to Red Cross messages. But most of the traffic that comes through Bob's machines is secret. To handle this fantastic array of information, the Army relies on computers. This reliance has given rise to one of the phenomenons of the Vietnam war; air conditioners on the battlefield. The computers are all highly sensitive to heat, dust and moisture, yet are used far out in the jungle. As a result, in some areas the soldiers may be living in tents and fox holes, yet go to sleep at night to the hum of air conditioners taking care of the delicate communication equipment.

Another sensitive job for Sgt. Bunch is handling many of the Vietnamese workers who perform various tasks around the Battalion headquarters. "The people remind me a lot of when I first went to Korea," says the veteran of that police action.

"When they first come into camp here it's a lot like taking a city boy out and trying to teach him how to farm. They don't quite know what we want them to do." Bob likes the Vietnamese pretty well and says the language barrier is probably the biggest problem he and the other Americans have in trying to deal with the local population. "Most of the Vietnamese want to work, and will work hard. Especially the younger ones," he says.

Bob looks out from his office to the big, brooding Vung Chau mountain that shadows the 41st signal battalion's headquarters. "Other than the people," Bob says, "this is an entirely different war. People shouldn't make comparisons. In Korea the mountains were higher and more barren and it was cold. Of course, we've got the jungle here to make up for any deficiencies in discomfort."

Qui Nhon has been under a lot of alerts but has never been attacked by the Vietcong since Bob got here last October. "And let's hope it stays that way," he says. His men perform tasks that keep them under a pretty good strain. So, he and Sgt. Major Don Buchanan of Batesville have helped their troops build a basketball court and a tennis court and they have a movie theatre under construction.

Bob and Sgt. Major Buchanan usually retreat to their own little recreational facility when their day's work is over. In the back of their barracks, on the second floor, they have requisitioned a twenty by fifteen foot room and equipped it with an icebox, plenty of cold beer and soda, and, would you believe, an air conditioner. Of course, when it gets right down to it, maybe sergeants with twenty years in the Army are pretty delicate too. Their main entertainment in their hideaway is just sitting and listening to all the stories that the guys back from R&R have to tell. "We hear some pretty funny stuff," laughs Bob.

Bob's wife, Elizabeth Klober Bunch, and their four children, Judy, 19, Peggy, 15, Bobby, 8, and Davie, 7 are all waiting for him to come back and take them fishing. Meantime 1st Sgt. Bunch has the Arkansas flag that Governor Rockefeller sent him, and the Ft. Smith Southwest American to keep him in touch with his home state.

Yeoman 2nd Lee Smith of Little Elm is proof that it is possible to make a year in Vietnam a rewarding experience. The former high school fullback joined the Navy on April Fools day 1964; he arrived in Vietnam in January of this year and has had six extremely busy months since then.

His job with the Navy is as a file clerk and typist in the office of Operations and Plans headquartered on the Danang River. The job is one of those mundane, but necessary tasks that abound in every war. But it's in his free hours that Lee really lives. A deeply religious young man, the twenty-four year old Arkansan takes his day off each Wednesday to teach English and Bible school at a war orphanage in Danang. Lee hs a degree in theology from The University of the Pacific, and he says his time with the 146 orphans "is a really rewarding experience." Built by the World Vision Mission of the Southern Baptist Church Association, the orphanage is now being expanded with a chapel and sanctuary.

Through his work at the orphanage, Lee has more contact with the Vietnamese people than do most Americans serving here. "It's certainly a different kind of contact with them than the Marines have out there," he smiles nodding towards the rice fields and mountains across the river. "On the whole I find the people very friendly and warm hearted, but of course there's always an ounce of suspicion."

"Our biggest problem is with the Confucianists," Lee says of his work at the Christian mission. "Their religion teaches them to concentrate more on themselves than on others and they don't believe in an after life.

They seem to think we're trying to exploit them, and I guess they have grounds for suspicion. They look at the history of their country. But all in all, they really don't know what we're after—maybe that's because they don't know what this whole war is about. The majority of the people don't seem to understand it."

But the people "seem to be searching for something" and Lee hopes the church might "help them overcome communism." In the meantime, he believes his work at the mission and a friendly hand and a smile is worth the effort.

The only things Lee has really missed have been his fiancee Loy Gregory of Miami, Oklahoma, and, "the simple things,— driving a car, seeing a movie, worshiping in my church." Being away from the states hasn't dulled his energies. On the nights he doesn't work he goes to the library provided by the Navy to take part in a study session conducted by the Chaplain. The discussions range from world politics to music. Lee does more than just talk about music; he also sings in a quartet that has been formed. Brushing back his long brown hair he says, "You have to keep active in everything. We can't let ourselves deteriorate."

The sailor from the Ozarks kept busy before he came to Vietnam too. He went to the University of the Pacific on a football scholarship and played four years of ball there as their fullback. Ask him how his team did, and he'll smile hugely and suggest you talk about something else. During college he worked for the United States Forest Service—and learned to speak Navajo to boot.

He'll be out of the Navy in a year now, and then he's heading back to Arkansas to set up an appliance business in Fayetteville or Ft. Smith. But while looking forward to returning to the States, he speaks soberly of the atmosphere he will return to. "Those riots back home are really distressing. If we can't maintain peace and harmony there, it seems silly to be 12,000 miles away in Asia trying to 'free' someone else."

Working side by side with Lee in Danang are two other Arkansans: Denzil C. Browning, son of Mr. and Mrs. L. G. Browning of Crossett, and Burris Clemons, 20, husband of Carolyn Sue Enlow Clemons of Bearden, and son of Mr. and Mrs. Earl B. Clemons of Thorton.

Yeoman 2nd Browning is bossman in the operations and plans office. He has a big staff "of three people" he laughs. The big freckled Arkansan has been in the Navy since July of 1961. "I graduated from Crossett High School in '57" he says, and then went to work for the paper mill as a "broke beater". He continued in that job until the draft started looking his way —"I was twenty-four, what could I do?"— and then joined up. Oddly enough, he spent the first five years of his term as a salior in Albuquerque, New Mexico . . . "working on weapons evaluation", he explains. Browning's time in Vietnam is almost up now. He's been here since September of last year and has worked steadily at his six day a week, 12 to 18 hour a day job. His only break came when he went on R&R to Bangkok, Thailand, a highly popular vacation land for all the servicemen here.

Like most Americans, Browning hasn't much time to mix with the Vietnamese. What little contact he does have comes at the Take Ten Club, a Navy entertainment center for the sailors in Danang. "I'll say one thing for the people here", he grins, "they seem to have a sense of humor." At the Take Ten the waitresses are always pulling something on the guys. They'll stick signs on our back when we're not looking, or unscrew the salt shakers so it spills all over the place when we try and use it. In the long run, I guess it makes the club a little more relaxing."

Denzil explains that the Navy's biggest job in Vietnam is not so much active combat as it is trying to keep the 400,000 plus men here fed and clothed. Denzil's office on the river is housed in a huge colonial monstrosity popularly named the "White Elephant". Two smiling, trumpeting white elephant figurines on either side of the gate greet the visitor. Both the building and his job bear the name because neither is something anyone particularly wants. The Operations and Plans Office "manufactures the logistical support plan", says Denzil. Which means their job is to figure out how to get food, equipment, and men distributed properly across the northern quarter of the country. The Navy supplies the Army, Air Force, and Marine Corps in addition to its own personnel, and as in any government office, that means "a heck of a lot of paperwork", groans Denzil.

Downstairs from Browning and Smith is where Burris Clemons of Thorton is spending his second tour of duty in Vietnam. It's really only his first year actually in Vietnam, but he spent nine months off the coast of this country in 1965 while he was serving aboard the USS Enterprise.

A 1964 graduate of Thorton High School, Burris married his wife, Carolyn Sue, just three days before he entered the Navy. Since then, he's had only twenty days home. But this month, he'll be flying to Hawaii to meet his wife for his R&R. "She's all I really miss," he says.

Though Clemons is a "paper soldier" too, he was sent to Survival Escape Rescue Evasion School (SERE) in Coronado, California before coming out. "Since we were coming to a combat zone I guess they felt we should be prepared just in case. So we spent a week on the rifle range, and then they put us out in the boonies for a week to dig up our own chow. "Oh yes", he recalls," we play 'prisoner of war' too. We act like we are escaped prisoners and they send 'guards' out to catch us. Of course everyone gets caught," he laughs.

While waiting for his tour in Vietnam to end, Burris works out at a gym on the beach and occasionally goes to the monthly boxing matches there. When he gets back home he wants to go to vocational school in welding and auto mechanics. Then Burris wants to set up his own shop and be his own boss back in Thorton, of course; there's no other place."

1st Lt. Bill Wells of Harrison held his captured Vietcong weapons, an old French carbine and a nine millimeter Beretta pistol. Being in Vietnam has resulted in a re-evaluation of things for me," he said. "I guess I've adjusted my priorities. A lot of things that I used to think were essential seem almost meaningless now. It's the little things—going home to my wife in the evening, hot meals three times a day—the things I used to take for granted are now vitally important to me and I think it will mean a better life for me."

After six months in Vietnam, Bill, the son of Mr. and Mrs. Joe Wells formerly of Harrison, now living in Republic, Missouri, has just returned to Cu Chi, Vietnam from a five day vacation with his wife, Kay, in Honolulu. The worst thing about being here, says Bill, is "being away from my family. That trip to Hawaii to see Kay was one of the best things I've ever done." His wife will meet him again in January when Lt. Wells leaves Vietnam, and starts making plans to use his degree in accounting.

Bill presently is the supply officer for the 2nd Battalion, 27th Infantry, 25th Division, but his first four months in Vietnam were spent on the line as platoon leader for the 1st platoon of Charlie Company . . . part of the Wolfhounds. On May 16th Lt. Wells and his platoon went on a helicopter assault, called an Eagle flight, into the center of the 269th Vietcong Battalion. The landing zone for Bill's helicopters was "hot", (that is, under enemy fire) that afternoon and his men had to fight their way across a canal into a field, and then take cover from the intense fire coming from a hedgerow and bunker complex in front of them. Suddenly, a machine gun and BAR opened up on his men from the flank. Immediately Lt. Wells took eight men, braved the fire, and knocked out the weapons threatening his platoon.

His fast action won him a Silver Star and Vietnamese Cross of Gallantry.

Bill discounts the medals. He says, "It's easy for an officer to get a medal for something like that. Men are doing the same thing I did all across Vietnam every day, but most of them don't end up with a medal." Although Bill is no doubt proud of his medal, he doesn't dwell on it. Instead, the 1966 University of Arkansas graduate talks mostly of an officer's concern for the safety and welfare of his men. "I guess my greatest fear when I was on the line was getting someone killed because of a stupid mistake. And the worst thing for the men, is the continuous operations in all kinds of terrain—being wet and tired for a month or two at a time."

Yet, Lt. Wells says the morale of the men is excellent. "Watch the men heading out into the field . . . laughing, joking, carrying on, they have really high spirits. The men have the attitude that this war is just something that has to be done. You come and do your share and go home—someone else comes and does their share." The twenty-three year old Arkansan believes "success" is the greatest morale booster for the men here. "If we go for a long time with no contact then the morale gets low. But if we go out and kill a lot of VC, take only a few casualties ourselves, get some weapons, et cetera, then the morale goes up."

Do the anti-war demonstrations back home bother the men, or are the soldiers even very much aware of them? "The main thing the men are concerned with", says Wells, "is hot chow that night . . . immediate things. They're interested in what concerns them, not the world."

Bill does have his own feelings about the war protestors however, "I wish the people back home who think the war is wrong would realize there are people dying here so they can have the right to protest."

On the other hand, Lt. Wells thinks there is a misconception about the intensity of the war here. "Probably 80% of the men in Vietnam won't hear a shot fired in anger. Of course the war varies around the country. For example, we don't have as many casualties from small arms and mortars as we do from booby traps. But, the important point is, that a lot of families back home are needlessly worried just because their sons or husbands are over here. All the press reports is the violent aspects of the war, but in reality, the vast majority of the men here are pretty safe."

As for the Vietnamese, Bill, says the average man "doesn't seem to care much about what's going on around him."

"They are a fairly simple people," he says, "basically honest. If the guy is not a VC he won't help you . . . but he won't hurt you either. He just wants to be let alone to farm his land."

Right now Bill's job leaves him a good bit of free time and a chance to rest a bit from his time on the line. As support platoon leader, his job is to find out where Intelligence wants the men to go, and what Operations wants them to do, and then provide the men with the trucks, mortar rounds, ammunition, food and endless other battle necessities that will enable the job to be done. The hardest part of his job is just trying to anticipate the needs. "Our tactical situation is very fluid, always changing, and it's a little hard to keep on top of it," he says.

Lt. Wells is a 1962 graduate of Harrison High School. While a high school student, he worked part time for Piggly Wiggly and Phillips Grocery. His wife, Kay, is the daughter of Mr. and Mrs. Glenn Davidson of Harrison.

The Michelin Plantation August 7

"Doc" Coffman, Medic with the 3rd Bde, 25th Infantry, took one last deep breath of good clean air in the clearing where the helicopters had brought in the food supplies, then waded into the dark, stagnant pool of jungle where he and his platoon live. He followed the faint track left by a tank in some previous foray through this wet, soft, poisonous land to the shelters being set up for the night. Lifting his helmet from the thick swatch of clean blonde hair that cushions his heavy iron "pot", the twenty year-old Medic settled into the mud, rocked back on his heels and stared with avid curiosity at the bare feet of one of his fellow soldiers.

"You've got to keep putting powder on those feet or you're going to have real trouble", he said to his ragged patient.

"The only trouble I've got is Vietnam," the young soldier replied.

With those words, Doc stood up and continued making the rounds until he could stop to eat some supper and lay down in the mud to sleep.

"Doc" is Richard L. Coffman, son of Mr. and Mrs. Walter G. Coffman of Jonesboro; basketball player, frog gigger, archer, youngest of nine children. One wonders what marvelous machine, or personnel officer, manages to unerringly select such quiet, dedicated, universally well liked young men to care for the wounded and sick in our wars. Standing six feet two inches tall, with a quick smile, but already sad eyes, Doc Coffman is well liked by everyone who knows him here. His Lieutenant says, "He's as fine a Medic as I've ever seen. The troops like him. He does a real good job."

A 1965 graduate of Brookland High School, Doc went to Arkansas State University on a basketball scholarship, did well in his studies, and started at guard on the junior varsity team.

But, for various reasons, he left college in the spring of his freshman year, was drafted, ("Well, I didn't want to go—but felt it was my duty so I did") and after basic training at Ft. Polk, Louisiana, that perfect introduction to the weather, terrain, and creatures of Vietnam, he went to Ft. Sam Houston, Texas for ten weeks of medical training. "They trained us in the basic requirements of first aid, but you really don't learn it until you get over here."

Doc got over here last February. Since then he's spent a lot of time in the jungle, and seen too many men die. But, as his Lieutenant points out, "we take more casualties from Vietnam than from Vietcong". A typical day in his life involves more of a fight with Vietnam than with the enemy. This is about how it is:
Late afternoon, Tuesday.

The one hot meal a day that the army tries to provide for its men in the field has arrived by helicopter, and Doc has carried his paper plate filled with sweet potatoes, ham, bread, and beans to his hootch to eat. There's no place dry to sit so most of the men, Doc included, place their helmets on the ground and balance on them gingerly.

The clouds are already building up for the fifth or sixth time today, but no wind finds its way through the thick foliage, and the men eat with their food a wet mixture of sweat, kicked up mud, and drops of accumulated moisture from the gray-green canopy over their heads. The men talk quietly as they sit around in various stages of undress. "Doc" sees to it that each man takes turns removing his boots, airing his feet for thirty minutes, and putting on clean socks.

Hanging his ten pound medical kit over his shoulder, "Doc" stoops from man to man spreading ointment here, foot powder there. "It's one of my biggest problems," he says, "trying to keep a full supply of ointments for all the rashes and things." He nods towards a big, hairy young soldier whose shirt is off. The boy's stomach is covered from his belt line to his lower chest with huge, angry red welts. "That's bamboo poisoning," says Doc. "It's a lot like poison ivy, itches like mad, won't cure up as long as he stays in the jungle. And there's no way to avoid it, really. It will work its way right through your clothes . . . and will end up looking like that". He points to the forearm of a soldier digging a hole. A patch of oozing, pus-filled sores the size of a man's palm glared out at the jungle. "We'll have to send him to the rear for a couple of weeks sometime soon."

In addition to the bamboo poisoning, Doc faces immersion foot, a disease of the foot caused by constant exposure to moisture that results in the skin becoming soft, swollen, sore, and, essentially, unserviceable; athletes foot, and the infamous jungle rot of World War Two fame.

Doc finishes his sick call just as the dark begins to settle in along with the rain. The paper plates from dinner are tossed into the six feet long and four feet deep holes that will provide some sort of protection for the men in case of attack during the long night.

Dark: Tuesday, Wednesday:

By 2000 hours (eight o'clock) the rain is coming down hard, and "Doc" is laughing because he chose the dry side of the hootch. The hootch is nothing more than two rubber ponchos joined together and stretched out a few feet over the ground to provide cover from the rain. A rainstorm in the jungle at night manages to work up a strong enough wind to penetrate into the thick mess. After the rain is the only time the jungle smells fresh. The rest of the time the air is too thick with the rich fragrance of living plants and the odor of dead and dying ones.

Doc and most of the other men have green air mattresses that make their nights sleep drier and more comfortable. "It's the best pound and a half of weight I carry in my pack," he says. The men who didn't bring one, or whose mattresses have leaks, sleep on extra ponchos. They roll each side of the poncho around sticks, so they end up with a framework of logs that allows the water to run under the poncho on which they sleep.

Night comes. The men drift off to a fitful sleep. But the empty looking, yet seemingly crowded jungle produces enough noises to make the sleep extremely light. Every few hours the guard changes. The raindrops crash to earth through the bushes and inevitably awaken the sleeper, who is certain he is about to be faced with a human wave assault, but he is usually only met with a faceful of wet leaves and rain. With the clouds and the thick jungle, it is totally black outside. The radio whines occasionally as the company commander calls to check the safety of each of his platoons.

One sleeper reaches over his head to the pack he is using as a pillow to make sure no water is finding a way in. A horrible clak! of teeth smacks into his hand. His whole arm numbs from the pain. Muffling a cry of rage and agony, he jerks his hand back and slaps at his attacker. In the blackness he can see nothing, but he feels his other hand crash into a large furry insect. Writhing on his poncho, he knows it was only a red ant that has bitten him. But it felt like a rattlesnake. "Maybe it was a snake," he muses, and then sits and waits to see if he is going to die a horrible death in that black night. But the pain subsides and his arm still works, so he reassures himself it was just an ant. Then, as his breathing and heartbeat return to normal, he wonders if there are more of the ants on the other side of his pack, taking refuge from the rain. What if they decide to come all the way in the tent? What if they're creeping over the pack towards his ear right now? He bolts up, lies down, switches ends, and finally sleeps.

Daybreak, Wednesday:

It is still black when the men begin to awaken, and they continue to doze in the quiet morning stillness that is broken only by the sounds of a few birds and a monkey patrolling their territories and having a look at the grumbling creatures below them. As the first light fights its way into the jungle, the soldiers crawl stiffly to their feet, talk softly, and then sit and open their morning breakfast of c-rations. The coffee is wretched but hot, and the only food that is really enjoyed at that time of the morning is some of the canned fruits. The Lieutenant tells one of the men to put his shirt on, his white skin shows too sharply against the green jungle. A shirtless Negro laughs when the same order is given to him, but he puts his shirt back on. "Doc" helps the radio operator get his heavy pack on, then loads his own equipment on his pack, and prepares to march out.

"Doc's" platoon will be the point today . . . breaking a pathway through the jungle, and prepared to take the brunt of an enemy attack. As Medic, Doc will be kept towards the rear of his platoon ready to move forward if needed. "The first time a man yelled 'Medic', I didn't have time to think about it—it was just an automatic reaction. I didn't get scared until afterwards."

"Doc's" responsibilities in the field are awesome. Not only must he brave all enemy fire to treat a wounded man, but he is also the man who must determine whether a wounded soldier is in such serious condition that a helicopter must be called in to med-evac him. As Harry Trumann used to say, "the buck stops here". It is the judgement of Richard "Doc" Coffman that will decide whether a man lives or dies, whether a helicopter crew will risk their lives to hover over the jungle and lift the man out.

"Hey Doc, did you mail my letter yesterday when the choppers came in?" asks one of "Doc's" buddies.

"Done" smiles Doc.

"Great", the other soldier says.

"Doc" fell into line and the march into the jungle began. There are paths and roads here and there in the jungle, but it is certain death to follow those booby trapped routes.

A thousand yards from the nights encampment, the jungle is close and clutching. The only sounds are the stumblings of the soldiers, and, far ahead, the sound of the point man hacking a path with his machete. The platoon passes a huge crater left by a thousand pound bomb, and walks by a pile of Hamm Beer cans and empty c-ration cans, testimony to previous operations here. "Those things should be buried", notes Doc. "The VC will gather that stuff up and use it in their booby traps."

The sunlight glints on the painted warriors that decorate the sides of each mans helmet. The warrior is the battalion sign, and each company has a different colored silhouette. Alpha company's is red. Doc's helmet is unmarked, except for the elastic band on the helmet that holds the camouflauge cover in place. On it he has written: Mom and Dad/Aunt Ruth/Micky Davenport. Micky, the daughter of Mr. and Mrs. Robert Davenport of Brookland, is his girl he explains. The soldiers continue their stooped march . . . seldom finding an opening large enough to stand up straight.

An hour later, covered with sweat and smelling like a goat, "Doc" jabs a finger at the ground as a warning. Half buried in the soft earth is the gray finned cannister of an unexploded rocket. Further on, just before taking a rest, he points to a piece of toilet paper that has been draped on a twig to warn of a red ant nest there.

Resting against a tree, Doc tells of a friend who jumped into a hole during a mortar attack. The hole was full of ants and the friend unhesitatingly opted to be out of the hole and risk the mortars rather than be in the hole with the ants.

He also tells of the time, his Sgt. killed a cobra with his machete. "It jumped up at him like a little dog, trying to bite him."

Noon:

After fifteen minutes rest, the platoon is up and off again. The battalion will be making only a short march today, about three miles. So the men will have all afternoon to set up camp.

Finally a clearing is reached, where the helicopters can bring in food, water, and supplies for the battalion. Waiting to find out where his platoon will be placed, Doc watches a scout dog stretched out nearby. "Those are really fine dogs," he says. "What gets me, is that after we get through with them over here, they are put to sleep. A few of them are used as blood donors for other wounded dogs, but most are put to sleep. We should be able to do something better than that for them."

Doc distributed salt pills to several of the soldiers. The soldiers joked as they dug their holes, put up their ponchos, and cursed the rain that was again falling.

"I guess the thing I miss the most," says Doc, "is just being in a dry place when it starts raining". The men took turns chopping away at the soil where the hole was growing. "The guys over here are real close to each other—as close as brothers. We live together, eat together, work together, die together. I'm proud to be able to do my part for them."

When Doc Coffman gets back to Jonesboro next year, he wants to go back to basketball, and continue his major in physical education and minor in history.

As for now, "Being here has really helped me; it's given me a sense of responsibility. I think I can face a lot of problems of life now that were awfully hard before. And, I guess most of all, I'm just proud to have even this limited association with medicine. I'm real proud to be a medic."

An ancient volcano, the massive, fog-shrouded Nui Ba Den Mountain, juts abruptly from the flat farmlands of Tay Ninh Province fifty miles west of Saigon. Vietnamese legend tells of a woman, Ba Den, who climbed the mountain grieving the loss of her husband in one of the many wars fought in this country during the past two thousand years. At the top of the mountain, she committed suicide, hoping that her proximity to the heavens would allow the gods to witness her death and immediately reunite her with her dead husband.

Standing at the base of Nui Ba Den, or Black Virgin Mountain as it is sometimes called, Captain O. Preston Williams can see only the scrubby banana trees, gray, torn rocks, and splintered tree trunks that litter the area around the rock crusher which his company guards. "This is a rest for my men," he says. "They've been in the field for ten months and this is the closest thing to relaxation that they've had. In two more days we'll be going back to the jungle again."

But for a few days, Preston has the luxury of sleeping in a tent, on a cot, with a floor of crushed rock from the mountain. The mountain is interesting in itself. From its 3,202 foot summit, all rivers and roads in the area can be seen . . . if the clouds below don't block the view. For years the mountain has had great military significance. It's peak has been occupied by the Japanese, the Viet Minh, the French and the Vietcong. Presently, the peak is controlled by the United States Special forces; the base is controlled by Captain Williams; and the in between is still controlled by the Vietcong.

Preston's major responsibility while he is at the mountain, is to guard the rock crusher. In the soft fertile land of the delta, a source of good crushed rock for road beds, mortar pits, cement manufacturing and dozens of other uses is a valuable possession.

Philippine and Australian troops regularly haul out truckloads of the mountain as do the Americans and Vietnamese for use as far away as Cam Rahn Bay, 120 miles northeast of Saigon.

So flat is the land around the mountain, that merely by stepping up on the fender of a jeep, the golden glow of the huge Cao Dai temple near Tay Ninh city, 15 miles away can be seen. The side of the mountain is used by Captain Williams men for target practice and weapons testing in the evenings, and the grinding crash of the rock crushers, and deep hollow boom of TNT, gives way to the sharp cracks of fifty calibre machine-guns, the screaming double booms of the recoilless rifles, and the violent explosion of the 81 millimeter mortars sending their steel fragments slicing into the breast of the Black Virgin.

Captain Williams arrived in Vietnam on Thanksgiving day, 1966. He hopes to leave a few days early this November so he can spend a very real Thanksgiving with his wife, Gayle, and their two sons, Brent, 3, and Blake, 6 months, (whom Preston hasn't seen yet) at their home in Jonesboro.

The twenty five year old Army Captain, son of Mr. and Mrs. O. P. Williams, Sr. of Pine Bluff, was first assigned as assistant intelligence officer for the 3rd brigade of his division in the town of Dau Tieng just below the vast War Zone C.

Dau Tieng used to be a sleepy little town, where the manager of the huge Michelin rubber plantation had little to do but harvest the rubber, swim in his pool, have a cool drink on his shady lawn, and ride his horse across the neatly planted land. Of course, he also had to turn his eyes from the regular loading and unloading of Vietcong guns and supplies that took place at the river dock near the heart of town in broad daylight . . . and he had to turn his pocket to pay the taxes the Vietcong collected from him, but altogether it wasn't a bad life.

Today, Dau Tieng and the Michelin plantation house a full brigade of the 25th Infantry division. By beginning his tour in Vietnam, as an intelligence officer, Preston was given the advantage of having a chance to really get to know his enemy and the territory around him before he went out to fight with a rifle company. Interrogating prisoners, flying all across the area each day, studying reports from the agents and paid informers he used to keep track of VC movements, Preston was well aware of the heavy arms shipments that crossed the border from Cambodia into Vietnam; the huge base camps and training centers located in War Zone C, the airport across the Cambodian border that served as a supply base for the VC; the occasional Red Chinese officer advisor that would be captured.

The plantation itself was Preston's greatest worry then. Most of the workers on the plantation were in collaboration with the VC, and it was and still is dangerous to venture even a little ways into those seemingly innocent orchards. "The Vietcong would put certain areas of the plantation off limits to the workers from day to day," says Preston. "Our agents reported what was off limits pretty regularly, and the managers of the Michelin had a big layout map of the plantation to keep us informed where their workers were each day. The Vietcong control of the area has been so complete, that part of the plantation is used as an R&R center by the 272d Regiment of the 9th VC Division." And as if that were not bold enough, Preston remembers that on the 23rd of March this past spring, the Vietcong gathered up all the people from several settlements within the plantation, moved them just outside of artillery range and held a big propaganda session with films of Vietcong victories, songs, the whole works.

"Whenever we would move into the plantation on an operation, the VC would follow right behind us," says Preston. "And when we leave Charlie comes in; the people get the point. We're only there for a short while, but Charlie can always come back."

But things aren't all milk and honey for the VC here. Small ambush squads are almost always left behind in the wake of U. S. movements in the area now. One ambush left behind while Captain Williams was in intelligence, killed a Vietcong captain, lieutenant, and first sergeant, who had been mapping U. S. movements. "They just got a little too cocky," says Preston.

On another occasion, a U. S. ambush set along a road near Dau Tieng heard people moving down the road. When they were in range, the Americans exploded a claymore mine. "We'd killed a woman VC organizer, as it turned out" says Preston. "She was about twenty five; the mine had torn off the top of her skull and her brains were laying in a puddle there in the road with her little blue hair ribbon stretched out across them. In her pockets we found photographs, and a list of names. She was from Hanoi. We had really wrecked their setup that night."

Preston remained as assistant brigade intelligence officer until May, then he finally got the command of a rifle company which he had been seeking since the past January. "The commander of a rifle company has the best job in Vietnam," Preston says firmly. "Working in a staff job, you can't exert too much influence, but as a company commander you become planner, improviser, and doer . . . that equals real solid responsibility, and I enjoy it. "In addition to that, Preston is considering making a career of the Army, and he thinks that in order to be "a half way decent senior officer" an Army man needs the battlefield command experience.

So far he's done a good job with his company. Since May his company is the only one in the brigade with an enemy body count. "We've killed eight VC confirmed, and have another six "probables"—that is, adding together the events of the fight, and blood trails and bandages we would find later, we can feel pretty certain we killed that other six even though we didn't find their bodies."

During his first nine days out with his company, Preston had contact with the VC every day. His three most frightening experiences came in rapid succession. On one he took his company over to the village of Xa Dinh Phuoc in the plantation to form a cordon and search the area. "But at the road intersection closest to the village we walked into a thick area of punji pits and booby traps. I had four men wounded in just a matter of seconds. So, choosing discretion, I backed off. I have a particular aversion to those darned things."

A few days later, Captain Williams was in the plantation again. Moving along carefully, he heard a burst of machine-gun fire from the rear of his company. The men there reported they had just glanced back over their shoulders and seen three VC waving at them: but the VC had escaped into the trees. "Soon after that, my lead elements reported they were looking at a whole bunch of 'rubber workers' all dressed in green uniforms moving across a clearing up ahead. I realized that they weren't rubber workers and called for artillery on their position, but as I started swinging my men around to cut them off we ran into trouble.

"We were crossing a road; all my lead platoon had crossed, and the VC were obviously just waiting for me. As soon as my radioman and I got started onto the road a machine gun opened up on us. I jumped into a ditch on the far side of the road . . . the machine gun knocked the heel off my boot.

"I tried to send some men around to outflank that gun when a second VC machine gun opened up on us. Well, they were more of a threat to my company than the big group of VC we were after, and even though I knew the VC machine guns were just there to keep us away from the big group, I called in for the artillery to switch over to the machine guns. At the same time, I set up my own machine guns and we had a machine gun firefight for about twenty minutes. First one gun firing, the other answering; it was really something—and we won."

"Later we searched the area where the big group had been spotted and found a five gallon tin of medical supplies . . . drugs, bandages, hypodermics, everything."

But Preston's biggest fight came on June the 5th, while his company was operating all alone north of Dau Tieng in the jungle. "We had spotted two VC the night before," he recalls and I had all of my men being extra careful. Finally, we just had the feeling that we were real close to Charlie, and the lead platoon and my command group all got down on our stomachs and started to crawl. It was a good thing we did! In the next instant three claymores went off right in front of us but all the shrapnel went over our heads; then several VC machine guns opened up on us from bunkers.

"I was behind a pile of dirt and the bullets were smacking into the other side constantly. As the fight developed I figured I'd better let the Brigade know about it, but to my horror I couldn't get them on the radio. I couldn't reach anyone, and the fight was getting bigger. Then I remembered that we had a mechanized cavalry group operating further north of us and behind the enemy. I reached them, gave them the coordinates for an airstrike in our area so they could call in some planes, and then heard them tell Brigade they were coming down to reinforce us. That was good to hear!"

In the next few hours, Williams and his 170 men pushed through the original group of six bunkers and into a VC village of twenty two tin roofed huts, and six hundred yards of trenchlines and fortifications. Fortunately, the village was mostly empty . . . apparently its occupants were off in the jungle. The few people that had been there had been the object of a direct hit by the airplanes that had strafed the area.

Searching through the area, Captain Williams began to realize the magnitude of his find. On the other side of the first village was an even larger area. "They had wooden bleachers set up for lecture sessions," Williams recalls, "and we found silhouettes of men and tanks they used for target practice. Some of the huts had green leather stuffed easy chairs. There were documents, a five gallan can of mail destined for other VC units and for North Vietnam, goats, a small tractor—it was incredible."

Even then, Captain Williams knew his company had been fortunate to have run across the camp when it was relatively unoccupied. But two weeks later he was even more certain of his good fortune . . . another unit in the area found over 150 bunkers. What Captain Williams and his 170 men had been fooling with was a training area for a Vietcong regiment.

Williams has two brothers, Gene Stacey Williams, a senior at ASU and member of Lambda Chi Alpha fraternity, and Sterling, an 11th grade student at Pine Bluff Senior High School.

Cua Viet, August 20

As he neared the coast of North Vietnam, Burt Renager
eased the throttle of his Swift Boat Number 80 back a little
further. The boat slipped on through the black night and the
coast of North Vietnam was only a hundred yards away . . .
Burt looked up from the flickering radar screen and smiled,
"Welcome to North Vietnam," he said.

It was the second time that day that Burt had wandered
into North Vietnamese territory. The first time his boat had
been unceremoniously chased away by artillery fire from the
big North Vietnamese guns that are hidden in the mountains
above the DMZ.

The day had begun in Danang some 60 miles to the south
early that morning. Burt, the husband of Paula Kalder Renager,
and son of Mr. and Mrs. B. W. Renager, Sr. of West Memphis,
is the skipper of a Swift Boat, the modern day analogue to the
PT Boats of World War II fame. His primary mission is to halt
the infiltration of men and supplies brought down from North
Vietnam in junks and barges. Like many combat jobs, much
of the time Burt's work is dull . . . but in a deadly sort of way.
The order looks good on paper, but when you start pulling up
alongside one of those small ragged boats and you're waiting
for him to fire, and know that if he does, he's going to kill some
of your men before you can return the fire, the order takes
on a different complexion. Lt. (j.g.) Bob Griffith of Palmer-
ville, wounded in the stomach this summer while inspecting
junks, can testify to how frightening it is.

Burt doesn't have so much problem with that order today.
Previously his patrol area was much farther down the coast
near Cam Ranh bay, the huge and very permanent American
base and port. There were a lot of junks to search then and
most were just innocent civilian fishermen. There are thou-

92

sands of these junks up and down the coast, and Burt's men have searched over 2,500 of them in the past nine months. But, now that Burt is working the area around the DMZ, he can be pretty certain that when he sees a Vietnamese boat in the water it's not a friendly.

Lt. (j.g.) Renager had been in Danang for repairs and was anxious to head back north to his base at Cua Viet. Pulling out of the harbor at Danang he passed the hospital ship Repose and then threaded his 22 ton craft through the hundreds of freighters that serve as the bucket brigade for supplies to the northern half of Vietnam. Once out of the harbor he smoothly ran his craft up to 25 knots and settled behind the helm. The American flag on the boat was popping in the wind like a whip cracking and the waves were hammers slapping against the hull.

It's a four hour trip from Danang up to Cua Viet and Burt stopped enroute for a rendezvous with a destroyer to pick up some milk and fresh bread. Then he met another Swift Boat and the two craft rolled easily in the water while the men had lunch and watched the black and grey clouds from inland battles rise above the thin white beach and green trees.

"As soon as we get to Cua Viet I'll pull a mail box investigation, said Burt, "and then we'll make a quick run up the coast to the North before we have supper and get ready for the night patrol." He eyed his sandwich distastefully. "I'll probably have a letter from my mother. She keeps writing and talking about all that good corn and okra and black eyed peas! Man! she doesn't know how that tears me up!" He laughed, "you know, one of the most incredible things that has happened to me while I've been in the service has been the way the mail from my church follows me around. Usually, mail from home is all screwed up for a month or so after I move to a new duty station; it takes that long for everyone to figure out where I am. Of course, I'm always really delighted to get that first letter when I arrive at my new station. And, the first letter is always from my church, The West Memphis First Baptist Church. They're the only organization in the world that always gets the mail through to me no matter where I am—I think it must be an act of God," he laughed.

The fifty foot long Swift shoved its uniform grey hulk into Cua Viet two hours later. Burt's home is simultaneously luxurious and wretched; luxurious because the area was temporarily the home of a large construction company, and it left behind flush toilets, hot showers, and a plumbing system that allows the men to drink pure water from the sink faucett; wretched, because it's like being camped in the middle of the

Sinai desert. "The sand, the wind, . . . and getting shot at," moans Burt. "Those are the things that really get me down." Struggling through the deep oozing dunes he stumbled in the door of his wooden hootch, dropped into a canvas chair and began brushing sand from the table top . . . "Let me clean off the table and we'll talk," he said.

"I arrived in Vietnam back in March. I volunteered for the Swifts, and I'm really proud to be commanding one. It's a great job!" Burt, a 1963 graduate of Memphis State with a year of medical school at the University of Arkansas behind him, enlisted in the Naval Reserve in 1960. He was selected for Officer Candidates school in 1964 and the next year was in Asia working as communications officer and navigator on an LST out of Japan. He jumped at the chance to have the responsibility of his own command and went into training with the Swift boats in 1966.

Burt walked over to the two Japanese iceboxes in a corner of his hootch and pulled out cold Hamms bear for the other Swift boat officers sitting around. Sand was blowing in through the screen and settling on the bunks and tables, onto the tops of the freshly opened beers, and on a book case made from orange crates (filled with such books as The Dirty Dozen, Under the Volcano, Dr. Zhivago, Hawaii, and Arrowsmith). "The damn sand is in the food too," stated Burt. "It is everywhere." Looking at the books in the case he commented that his three favorites weren't there: Elmer Gantry, the Prophet, and the Catcher In the Rye.

A Captain came in and the other five skippers gathered around and planned their activities for the rest of the day. Burt was to make a short patrol north before the sun went down, and then come back in for chow before starting an all night patrol at eight o'clock. Burt grunted assent; someone opened a box of Dutch Masters cigars and Burt started down to his boat.

Approaching the dock he groaned; a Marine sergeant was loading a large loudspeaker on board. "Oh, God!," cracked Burt, "another night of psywar!" Sure enough, the Marine was a member of one of the psychological warfare teams and wanted Burt to run his boat along close to shore so they could broadcast appeals to defect to any North Vietnamese soldiers within ear shot. "Of course, if they are in ear shot of us, then we are within gun shot range of them," Burt said grimly.

The afternoon sunlight was strolling in the water as Burt moved out of the base and started up along the coast. From Cua Viet, it is less than five miles to the DMZ, and it is unhealthy to get too close to the shore. Burt's boat is heavily armed. It boasts three fifty calibre machineguns, an 81 millimeter mortar, and each of the six man crew is armed with an

M-16 machine gun. One of the crew members smiled, "Yeh, we're pretty well armed, but we aren't too tough. This ol' boat is all aluminum—the 'Reynolds Wrap Delight' we call it. A 22 bullet from my little brother's target rifle would go right through this thing!" Actually the boat is made of Alcoa Aluminum, and was originally designed to make runs to the offshore oil rigs in the Gulf of Mexico. Burt was racing along the coast pretty fast now; the psywar speaker started blasting out music . . . "If you miss the train I'm on, you will know that I am gone . . ." the notes drifted in towards the barren shore. There wasn't exactly a rush of deserters on the beach. Burt shrugged and kept moving along the coast, closer and closer in at the urging of the Marine. Then suddenly the air was filled with static, quiet, then a sharp curse from the Marine.

"That's about average," smiled Burt. "That speaker usually shorts out or quits pretty quickly."

Then, turning, his tone changed. "Let's go shoot 'em up." The boat crossed the southern edge of the DMZ and kept moving northward. Burt pointed to a ridge of mountains running out to the coast about ten miles ahead." "They have big guns up there," he said. They'll be watching us right now and when they think we're in range they'll open up. If they have surface radar to track us then we'll really be in trouble . . . but I don't think they do. They have to rely on eyesight to hit us . . . that's why I prefer to come up here at night."

Another Swift boat joined Burt's boat and the two craft took turns darting into shore firing their machine guns and their mortars in hopes of drawing fire from a target on the beach. Both boats fired blindly into the beach and the tree line. Clouds of dense white phosphorous boiled up from the trees as the mortar shells hit. The fifty calibres banged away up and down the beach tearing jagged holes in the trees. Nothing happened.

Burt's Swift and the other boat pulled back about 200 yards off shore and sat. The men loosened their flak jackets, smoked cigarettes, and talked. It was sharply quiet after the cacophony of the firing, and very peaceful.

Then a loud flat 'BOOM!' jumped across the water. For two aching seconds everyone stood paralyzed watching the geyser of water that had leaped into the air off the bow of the other boat. A second loud boom and another white spout of water jumped up . . . but by now both Swifts were moving out at full speed, leaving a cloud of black exhaust fumes where they had been standing. Burt, had his throttle all the way forward, and was throwing his speeding craft right and left. Those booms were from the North Vietnamese artillery. No foxholes to hide in out here! All Burt could do was run. More booms, more geysers of water, long agonizing seconds trying to urge the boat forward, forward, ever faster. The booms continued, but now they began to drop behind. Finally he was out of range. The race was to the Swift. He stopped his boat and everyone sat quietly for a few minutes before they began to talk of the attack.

Burt ran his boat southward. Cua Viet has dozens of small American flags flying from the many small boats anchored there. Each flag is at a different level for some reason and the whole base looks a bit like a filling station having a price war. The sun was almost down.

By eight o'clock the crew had been fed and was back on board; so was the psywar Marine.

The radar and the compass would be Burt's only means of directing himself now. A total blackout exists all along the coast and aboard all boats. Any exposed light might invite immediate attack by one side or the other. The Swift started north Burt moved it slowly through the water explaining that the ocean was so full of phosphorescence in this area that at higher speeds the wake of the boat was highly visible from the shore. The boat moved north in the South China Sea towards the Gulf of Tonkin.

Burt's eyes strained at the radar; sometimes a high wave would show up on the scope as a white blip and Burt would tense waiting to see if the blip would reappear. Nothing. Suddenly a bright dot showed on the screen; it stayed there; Burt watched it closely. "Airplane," he announced. "Look how fast it's moving across the screen." The boat moved on northward in the night.

The wind was warm and smelled good. "That's almost as good as the delta in the spring," said Burt. "This is a hell of a way to be spending a nice summer night." People ask me how this war is going . . . the whole thing makes me mad to talk about it. There's just no progress.

"I can't even develop too much sympathy for the Vietnamese people. A lot of them are damn glad there is a war—they have a good thing going and don't want us to stop. Lots of money being made by some of the people over here," he snorted.

The radar screen showed the coastline as a jagged white stretch, like chalk marks on a blackboard. A dark gap in the center of the DMZ showed a river mouth. As Burt watched the screen a blip appeared on one side of the river and slid silently across merging into the other bank. "That was a boat" stated Burt. We see that a lot, but we can't get to them in time to do anything. And, I wouldn't dare stick my nose into that river mouth."

The waiting began again. "October will be my month for R & R, he said. I'll be in Honolulu with my wife in no time at all. Then, it won't be long before I'll be home. I keep thinking of all the things I miss; Bill's Barbecue with Michelob on tap, and a football game on the TV; shaved legs and no stockings . . . seeing a good looking woman walking down the street, and just enjoying looking at her! It's going to be float trips on the White River . . . beer, fishing, tell a few war stories— and then back to school for me when I get home." The dots on the screen began to look like ping pong balls all of a sudden. They just came away from the coast, one, two, three, five, fourteen, fifteen. Those were junks! All moving towards a small island off the coast. "That's Charlie!" said Burt with excitement. Another Swift further ahead of Burt's boat began to call back to Cua Viet for permission to attack them.

The radio crackled . . . "Wait," it ordered. "Here we go again!" moaned Burt. The junks were almost halfway to the island now. Burt explained that he had to have permission to attack because the junks were in North Vietnamese waters and were not firing on him. The radio crackled again . . . perhaps a nearby destroyer could get permission to fire. Five minutes later came the same answer. "No."

"Well, how about an airplane," cried Burt. "Maybe we can get an airstrike on them." Some of the boats were now merging into the coast of the island. "We'll never make it" said Burt.

Time passed and Burt watched the junks disappear from the screen, unharmed.

The radio ordered Burt's boat back down towards Cua Viet to pick up two Marine scouts who had spotted some VC movement along the coast earlier. With the scouts on board peering intensely through an infrared telescope Burt cruised up and down for the rest of the night. Occasionally the psywar Marine asked to move in closer to allow him to make some broadcasts towards the shore. Burt just snorted—then, right before dawn, cruised back into Cua Viet, shook the sand out of his bed sheets and went to sleep.

Ty Kelsoe had his draft notice in his hand when he drove into Conway, in the summer of 1966, to join the SeaBees. "I knew I was going to have to go," says the 24 year old Arkansan, "and I heard the SeaBees would let me keep working as a carpenter." He was right.

Builder Second Class Kelsoe, whose wife, Mary Lynn, lives in Greenbrier, had been working for his father's construction company, building residences, ever since he graduated from Greenbrier High School in 1961. Today he is building Marine barracks and forward bases north of Danang.

Officially, the Seabees are listed as U.S. Pacific Fleet Naval Mobile Construction Battalions. They get their nickname from the first letters of the last two words. In wartime they provide military and construction support, and defense operations when necessary, for the Naval and Marine forces in Vietnam. Their motto is, "Constrimus, batuimus," which means 'We build, we fight!' Since World War II and Quadalcanal their spirit has been summed up as the "can do" outfit. Ty came into the SeaBees as an E-5, a skilled laborer, under the Direct Procurement Petty Officer Plan in '66. The Navy sent him to Officer Candidates School in Rhode Island for six weeks, and then on to Gulfport, Mississippi, and Camp Lejeune, North Carolina for training. During that time he and the other new SeaBees he was with got used to working as a team. In Gulfport, Ty built a teen center for the kids, and a bit further away constructed Girl Scout Camp Wiggins.

With that pleasant introduction to military life behind him, Ty and his battalion were off for Vietnam. "We arrived here in June," says Ty. "We moved as a battalion, never as individuals. So the whole battalion will stay here until the end of January. I'll just try to make the best of it."

98

Each branch of the military services in Vietnam has a somewhat different tour of duty in the country and the SeaBees are no exception. Ty will spend eight months in Vietnam and then his battalion will be rotated back to the States for five months rest before they are sent back to Vietnam again for another eight month tour.

Red Beach, where Ty is presently stationed is a fairly pleasant area. Situated on a lovely sandy beach, the base has green mountains rising up behind to offer shade from the late afternoon sun. His work is ten hours a day six days a week—and then, only six hours on Sunday. But, they told us when we came over,—Ty smiles—"all we're going to get out of this is self satisfaction."

His main work has been on Marine Barracks. "I like working on those barracks," says Ty, "but, we spend an awful lot of time remodeling places for officers clubs . . . and, I think some of that work is just plumb unnecessary. They're living pretty high on the hog as it is." One group of the men at Red Beach make a run over to a place called Marble Mountain whenever they have a chance. "That's really Charlie's country," Ty says, "but those guys wanted to go up to build an aid station for the Marine guards there."

Ty likes the country around Red Beach . . . and he has a real respect for the Vietcong. Looking out from his seat on a wooden pew in the grass and bamboo church the SeaBees have built, he points to Hill 724. "We get sniper fire from up there fairly often, no matter how many patrols we keep out. Those guys are tough! I respect those little fellows; they can slip right through these mountains and through our guard posts just slick as a button."

The men at Red Beach are not allowed off their small base, so they have to make their own entertainment, and recreation. The beach offers some swimming for them, and the ever popular baseball and football games have been supplemented by the construction of a slot car track.

The food, always a critical morale factor in any war, is great according to Ty. "It's like Christmas everyday!," he smiles. The chow hall at Red Beach, constructed by the men who eat there, sports almost fifty state flags. Along one wall are letters from the Governors of the states that sent flags. An Arkansas flag hangs from the ceiling and a letter from Governor Rockefeller has a place along the wall.

Looking ahead to January when he'll be back home, Ty says he misses his wife, Mary Lynn, the most. When he gets back home he just wants to be able to rest for awhile before he starts work again. While he's resting, he wants to catch up on his fishing and hunting. "The day before I went into the service, my brother and Dad took me to Lake Overcup, and we spent the whole day. We lost about nine dozen minnows catching crappie," he laughs.

Ty really hasn't had any problems since he arrived in Vietnam. In fact, he says he's learned a lot of new things about carpentry. "But, it's just like at home," he explains, "every carpenter has a different way of doing things . . . of course, it always ends up the same." Ty says the only problem they do have is that his men just "can't get it done as fast as the officers want it done." That is nothing new. In fact, it brings back the words of Douglas McArthur in a letter to Admiral Ben Moreell during World War II: "the only trouble with your Sea-Bees is that you don't have enough of them."

Ty has two brothers, Eddie, 16, a student at Greenbrier High School; and Drewey, 20, a student at Arkansas State College.

A little over two years ago, the United States Marines were setting up their first outposts on Hill 327 which overlooks Danang. They took few casualties in the process. Having gained that hill they had a spectacular view of the heartache that awaited them.

Today, when a Marine is wounded out there—away from the Hill—a helicopter will pick him up and medevac him to the Marine Corps 1st Medical Battalion. The helicopter will circle directly over Hill 327 with its bristling HAWK missles and begin to settle on to the pierced steel helicopter pad where Hospital Corpsman 3rd Class Lester H. King of Cash will be the first man he sees on his long journey to recovery.

King, a 1965 graduate of Grubbs High School, came to Vietnam by the way of Florida and Iceland. "When I got those orders to Iceland, I figured I had it made," he says. "But I ended up here anyway." King joined the Navy because he wanted into the medical field and the Navy seemed to offer the best program for his purposes. He arrived in Vietnam in January, 1967, and had a good introduction. "When I got off the truck in the compound," he recalls "I heard two loud explosions. I was scared silly . . . until someone told me that was just the R.M.K. Construction Company blasting a road up to the new officers club."

When Lester arrived, he worked fifteen hours his first day—and then only five hours the next day. Now his routine has settled down to an eight hour day with every other Sunday off. His job is to unload and assist in the care of the wounded brought directly in from the battlefield. The activity at the First Medical Battalion receiving room is a pretty good index of the tone of the war outside Danang—just as an emergency

101

room in any city is a good indication of the highway conditions on a holiday weekend.

Between casualties, Lester sits in a green wheel chair in the shade from the emergency room porch. He reads letters from home, listens to a baseball game or football game on a portable radio and takes it easy. "The busy, all-day-days are pretty far apart," he says. So he sits, and listens.

"We hear the choppers coming first. I can pretty well tell when the chopper is on its way in here or someplace else by the sound of its approach." When it is headed for King's office he turns into a flurry of action.

As the helicopter settles to the pad, he races the sixty paces out to the landing zone with a stretcher; two more men run with him; one to help with the stretcher, the other to hold high the plasma bottle which keeps the wounded marine hooked in to life until he reaches the operating room. Those precious seconds between the field and the operating room mean life or death. Lester and his helpers are blurs of action as they unload a wounded man and rush him to the receiving room. Even as they race away, the helicopter pushes off in a storm of wind and noise for another run to the battlefield. Across the pad, a small wooden bridge, a wooden ramp, and then into the receiving room go the wounded. There, on a stretcher propped between two sawhorses they begin to receive real medical help. Doctors in clean white gowns, but in dirty, bloody sneakers, peer anxiously at the wounded man to determine the extent of his injuries and the best immediate care to be given. The room has a normal capacity of twelve patients but could hold twice that number in a pinch.

"We just use the room for the emergency steps," says Lester. "After that we can send them on to the operating rooms. If the patient requires brain surgery or eye surgery we send him on out to the hospital ship or to the Navy hospital here."

Walking back down the wooden sidewalk while the patient is being cared for, the visitor is met by a gentle breeze from the rice paddies across the helicopter pad. The sidewalk itself is strewn with boots, a shirt, perhaps, a rifle from the wounded marine. A neat, deep box just at the edge of the pad was placed there to pile these items. In the box are the last vestiges of the Marines' battle with the enemy: canteens, a rifle, a bloody shirt and a shredded flak jacket, and a dented helmet. Once the Marine has left these behind, he need only worry about his battle with his wounds. Heat waves rise from the helicopter, pad, a chopper soars far overhead, and in the rice paddy a Vietnamese farmer tills his fields.

"We also treat Vietnamese wounded here," says Lester. "They are usually either Vietcong or Vietcong suspects."

Though it would seem that these Vietnamese would be terrified of being taken into the alien hospital, Lester says that they are very quiet and cooperate well. "The only problem is when the family of a victim shows up," says Lester. "That's our worst problem. 'Mamasans' come in crying and carrying on. They do more wailing than the injured man. And they are always in the way. We practically have to tie them to a pole to get them apart from the patient so we can work on him."

Since the Vietnamese are usually Vietcong suspects, an interrogator from one of the intelligence branches is there at his side as quickly as the doctor. While the doctor closes the wound, the interrogator tries to loosen the tongue of the suspect.

For Lester, the worst part of his job is to unload and treat the men who are double amputees, or are maimed, or are KIA —dead." We work hard on them—very often, though they are dead when we unload them. It's awfully sad," he says.

The men with really severe wounds are often in a great deal of pain; in that case, Lester says, the receiving room has a better pain reliever than medicine. "The Chaplain is always here to talk with the men as they come in, and, often, the Chaplain can calm the men and ease their pain more easily and quickly than any of our drugs. A wounded man is scared," says Lester, and the Chaplain can help him there."

And that's true. It is an interesting thing to see the Chaplain bent over a man with multiple shrapnel wounds, while Lester, blue eyes gazing intently through his glasses at a plasma bottle, physically keeps the man alive.

Lester says he misses his family and not being able to get to know the people off the compound. The first thing he wants to do when he gets back is go camping with his folks on the White River. He'll be out of the Navy in August of '69 and then he wants to go to college and train as a lab technician— though lately he's been thinking that he might want to be an anesthesiologist.

He's hoping he can continue to work in Danang and away from the battle. To describe his version of the battlefield, he points to a popular cartoon, SGT. MIKE, which hangs on the wall of the receiving room. The cartoon shows a wounded corpsman facing an angry Sgt. Mike who is yelling, "What to you mean you're wounded? You corpsmen are supposed to set an example!"

Lester is the son of Mr. and Mrs. Lester L. King of Route 1, Cash. He has a brother, Johnny, who is also serving in Vietnam.

Air Force Master Sergeant Troy Creamer of Harrison has an office that sits in the center of the busiest airport in the world . . . Saigon's Tan Son Nhut. Standing there in the late afternoon, watching the lights come on around the airfield and the setting sun gleaming on the white dome of a satellite tracking station, he said, "It's just like an assignment in the States." A sleek black Voodoo jet roared off the field headed for a reconnaisance flight over North Vietnam, and two flares shot into the air outside the perimeter." In fact, this is a better assignment than some I've had."

Well, Troy Creamer should know. He's been in the Air Force for nineteen years and has served from Texas to England to Alaska . . . though he's never been able to manage an assignment to Little Rock Air Force Base. Master Sergeant Creamer is now ending his tour of duty in Vietnam where he has been working as chief of the fuel cell repair shop at Tan Son Nhut.

Partially because the shop takes up so much space, and partially because he sort of wanted to get moved away from the formalities and officers that inhabit the edge of the base, Troy has his shop set squarely in the middle of the airfield. His buildings are an unimposing collection of spare parts thrown together to offer a little shelter from adverse weather. The 'office' has a worn yellow porch that offers a quiet place to sit for the many men who enjoy hanging around the shop even when they're off duty. In front of the porch is a popular horseshoe pit that is in continual use far into the night. The inevitable sandbag bunker squats to one side of the office. Behind the office is the real work area . . . a sign warns "Work Area, Do Not Call Attention."

The two most impressive features of the fuel cell repair shop are, first, the long white fuel cells themselves, and second, the finest looking outdoor toilet since Mamie Yokum was a little girl . . . The outbuilding is labeled: "Base Operations."

The fuel cells that Troy's men work on carry the extra fuel that enable the thirsty jet aircraft with which we fight this war to carry out their far ranging missions. Troy supplies reconnaisance planes exclusively at Tan Son Nhut." We're the picture getters here," he says. The planes that take off go all the way to China, take their photos and then run them home to be developed in the highly sophisticated photo labs at the airbase.

The 46 men who work for Troy are all easy going. Troy says he tries to keep it pretty informal and like a civilian job. "There's no need for any harsh military rules out here," he says. Troy is well liked by all the men." Heck, I've never been anyplace where I was without friends," he says. "I guess it's because I've never met anyone I was afraid to go up and talk with."

Troy says his job here is no harder than it was in the States. "Of course, I came from the Strategic Air Command, and they're practicing war all the time anyway," he smiles. The only work problems he has stem from the short tour of duty the men spend in Vietnam." Just as they begin to learn the ropes and get used to their jobs, their time is up and off they go and in comes someone new. . . ."

Walking back across the airfield to have dinner, Troy pointed at the new buildings ahead and the construction going on all around him. "When I came here this place still looked pretty barren." As Troy walked along, he said hello to several other Arkansas men who work at Tan Son Nhut: Big Joe Douglas from Newport; James Payne, husband of the former Patt Patterson of Conway; and Donald McCain, son of Mr. and Mrs. Edgar McCain of Manila.

Eating and drinking facilities at Tan Son Nhut are superb. Palm trees have been planted along the small streets inside the base; the buildings are freshly painted and clean. For the men Troy eats with, there are no less than five bars and four chow lines offering everything from cafeteria type food to a cook your own steak barbecue area. TV sets can be found in most common rooms.

"It's funny," he said. "We'll get some newly arrived airman who will come into the barracks and sit down and really worry about getting killed. They hear all these combat stories back home that just don't apply to us. The men go back home from here and people expect us to know all about what's going on; but in reality they know more about the place than we do . . . they've got lots of newspapers, and newscasts, and politicians. We just work most of the time and don't have a chance to look around much."

Troy went in to have a coke before starting home; over the bar is a sign that says "No one under 21 will be served." The sign seemed sort of absurd even if this was only the rear of a war area.

"When I arrived here last year," Troy says, "they didn't have enough room for us to live on base, and really no way of finding us places to live off base. We were just on our own. So, one day I just went through the gate and started wandering around looking for a place to live . . ." He turned down a narrow street, its oozing mud reflecting the neon lights of nearby bars. Smells of spiced food, sounds of GI laughter mixed in with family conversations in Vietnamese filled the dark air of the alley. "And I found this," Troy pointed ahead.

Troy rented a large room in a Vietnamese home. Two other rooms in the upper part of the house are also rented to Americans and the Vietnamese family makes a fairly handsome income from the rental. The family that owns the house lives on the ground floor. The Father is a man in his sixties who speaks Vietnamese and French and has learned a great deal of English in the last few years. He speaks very softly when he is speaking English and smiles at his twenty year old daughter, an airline hostess for Pan American. "When I was a young man," he smiles, "we would all learn French. But now we have a new era," he nods to his daughter, "her generation learn English."

Drinking the fine, hot greenish yellow Vietnamese tea that the Mother brought in, Troy explained his own fondness for the Vietnamese people. "They're like people anywhere," he says. "A GI comes along and the first thing the people want is his money. But once you get to know the people they're o.k. I've been living with them here for almost a year now, and they're much friendlier to me. You get to trust people after you get to know them a little. There's a mamasan down the way that sells cokes; sometimes I won't have any change in my pocket, but will want a coke. Why, I just go over and pick one up, tell her I'll pay her later and walk off. She just nods. She knows me now."

Troy laughed and stood up. His six feet plus frame filled the room. "Try and imagine yourself as a Vietnamese," he said. "You weigh sixty five or a hundred pounds and are padding along barefoot or in sandals down this little alley and all of a sudden you look up and here comes a two hundred and twenty five pound red faced monster wadding towards you. Well, wouln't you be just a little bit afraid to walk over and say 'howdy'? We sort of scare them."

106

"I'll be glad to get back to Harrison!" Troy turned and walked up the grey concrete steps to his wartime room outside Tan Don Nhut.

An American Marine moves cautiously along a trail with his company. They have been walking all morning in hopes of overrunning a Vietcong force. As the young Marine walks, a Vietcong sniper slowly adjusts the sights of a rifle and places the cross hairs on the head of the Marine. A few moments later, the Marine is dead; his company is on the ground scanning the unmoving face of the jungle for some twitch that will indicate the source of their threat. It will be at least half an hour before the Marines can move again . . . perhaps the company commander will call in an airstrike on the suspected location of the sniper before he risks his company further. In the meantime, the sniper will have disappeared.

The use of snipers to deny freedom of movement to an opposing army has been a favorite technique of warfare for as long as war has existed. The Vietcong have made particularly good use of snipers in Vietnam, much to the frustration of U. S. forces there. But, now, they are getting a taste of their own method. L/cpl. David J. Butt, son of Dr. and Mrs. W. J. Butt of Fayetteville, is one of the men who is dishing it out. He is a sniper.

"Butt's down at The Island," said the Marine Captain. Then he looked out the screened door of the company office and watched a man patiently stomping his way through the sand. An occasional breeze stirred the accumulated sand on the wooden sidewalks. "We lost a lot of people down there last week. They were coming back from a patrol and had a couple of their guys on stretchers, so they were kind of bunched together. As they came down this pathway down the side of a hill, they touched off a 150 millimeter artillery shell that was set up by the path."

108

"Hey, Sarge!," a corporal yelled from the bottom of the stairs leading into the company hut. "Truck's ready to go."

"Yeh, yeh. Just a minute. You got a passenger."

The captain walked away from the door to a map on the wall. His dark green tee shirt, stained dark and wet by his sweat, stretched as he pointed. "It was right in there. It was bad. Two of the men were decapitated by the explosion. The other eight that were killed died of traumatic amputations . . . legs and arms just blown away."

He leaned against the edge of his desk, piled with booklets describing the latest "lessons learned" in Vietnam. He fingered a letter in his hand and read a few more sentences. His voice choked a little. "This is from the parents of one of the men who were killed." Suddenly his eyes filled with tears. "I'll be down to see you later." He turned quickly and slipped into a rear room.

It took five minutes for the truck to back up in the soft sand; and then another ten minutes or so for it to slowly dig its way out of the compound and onto the rough asphalt road. The truck was filled with oranges, apples, milk, and water cans. In addition there were several dozen empty ammo crates to be used for general construction work at the various outposts. A large wooden sign declared: "This Road Has Been Swept For Mines." One of the men sneered as he read it.

"Shit!," these people know when there's mines planted on this road, but we never get told! Every morning we just have to get out the mine sweepers and walk it!"

The truck was picking up speed now and the marines were perched precariously atop the crates and food. They were obviously unhappy to be leaving the relative safety of the compound. The speed increased even more and the people along the road began to dodge out of the way. Helmets off, faces blank, broken fingernails digging at the orange skins, their bitterness was awesome as they rode the orange peel special.

"Look at that turd!" screamed a nineteen year old from New York. His mouth grabbed and mashed into an orange and the juice spilled down his chin as he watched an old man on a bike run off the road to avoid the truck.

The other marines began to smile. The road was heavy with people and the truck driver began swerving back and forth never slackening speed. Suddenly, they began to tear chunks of peel and fruit loose from the orange and throw them viciously at the Vietnamese. "You turd! You Turd! YOU TURD!"

Those who had not seen the truck coming would hear the noise just in time to turn and dodge an orange peel. The Marines were laughing . . . but without humor. The young Vietnamese tried to grab something to throw back; but always too late. The older men, and one pregnant woman just stared with obvious hatred.

At the Island the children were smiling. The truck had reached there after a twenty minute ride and the men were joking with the kids that swarm along the river as supplies are paddled across to the Marine camp. All trace of anger and apprehension on the part of the Marines was gone. They ate Vietnamese popsicles and played with the youngsters. A few laughed and cursed good naturedly at a mass of eight children in an aluminum rowboat. The kids were hand paddling back across the small stream that separates the Island from the road. The boat was used to ferry supplies across the fifty yard gap.

For the past year the Marines have thrown hundreds of patrols across the area and received in return for their efforts only hundreds of casualties from the booby traps that seem to grow there. They have killed only a few Vietcong suspects. The futility of patrolling the area led to the establishment of the outpost at the northern edge of the Island. Since the Marines can't use the Island, they want to make sure the Vietcong can't use it either.

Some patrols are still sent southward from the post; but they don't penetrate very deeply. Instead, a fifty foot tower has been constructed. From the top, a lookout or a sniper commands a view of the entire island. To the southeast, an American destroyer lay offshore; its big guns roamed freely up and down the battered free fire zone and the nasty black smoke was heavy all across the tangled splintered jungle.

Butt was propped against some sandbags beneath the tower. He turned to smile. His blue eyes were startling in the midst of his red sunburned face. Blonde hair bleached almost white by the sun, his eyebrows and lashes clung around his eyes like puffs of yellow smoke. He was surrounded by the sounds, smells, and intensity of five men blasting away at the jungle in front of them.

"We're covering for one of our patrols," he explained. Pointing to one side, "They'll be coming back in over there. Since Charlie thinks he's so clever with his booby traps we thought we'd show him what we can do. We found one of his traps out there and have boobytrapped his boobytrap. When he comes back to find out why it didn't go off. Well, he'll find out all right."

David Butt ended up in Vietnam, he says, because he "had an 'Uncle' who wanted him to go on a safari." The twenty year old sniper graduated from Fayetteville Senior High School in 1964 and then spent two years at the University of Arkansas majoring in education and English before he joined the Marine Corps.

"The sniper school was strictly voluntary," David explained. "They put up notices about it and I told them I was interested so they sent me up for an interview with the Lieutenant in charge of snipers who told me what it was like. I'd done a lot of varmint shooting when I was back home, so I felt as though I would do o.k. shooting. But, the Lieutenant wanted to know if it would bother me to see a man's face blown all to pieces and his guts fall out. With this telescopic sight, it's like being only a few feet away."

"Now that I've been doing this for awhile, it doesn't bother me too much. After you've seen so many Marines killed you want to see the enemy get his. So, when I'm successful the only reason I'm happy is not because I've killed a man, but because I've given him back some of his own."

David picked up his rifle, "a Remington Model 700 with a medium heavy barrel" and aimed across the wide expanse of field in front of him. "See the top of that house over there?" he asked. Far back into the jungle, more than five or six hundred yards, the orange red roof of a deserted house could be seen. David adjusted the rifle, settled it comfortably into his shouler and gazed long and hard through the Redfield 3 to 9 power accurange scope. "When you look at something a hundred yards away through this, it's like you were standing only ten yards away." He squeezed the trigger and a patch of red dust leaped up from the very end of the roof where he had aimed.

Walking back to his tent, he explained his job. "We work with all the companies in the regiment. When somebody needs a sniper to work their area they send word back and we come down for a few days. I've worked this whole place. The Horseshoe, The Hill, The Sand Dunes, The Mud Flats; but I like the Island real well. There's not so many VC around here. But the boobytraps make up for that; man, you can't go past the schoolhouse without hitting a boobytrap!"

David works in a team with another sniper on all assignments. His partner is Tim Dunn, from Staten Island, New York. The nineteen year old Dunn is a veteran sniper now, but had never fired a rifle before he joined the Marines.

Sometimes David works from a stationary position, like the tower at the Island, but usually he and Tim go out with a patrol. "The patrol goes out for our benefit," David explains. "They provide security for us. When I get into a position where I think I might spot someone, I sit down, get comfortable, and then scope out the area with my rifle . . . using it like I would a pair of binoculars.

111

"My targets are almost always moving and it's hard to hit them. I just have to sit there hour after hour, not moving . . . bugs eating me up . . . sun beating on me, or rain running down my neck . . . and wait. Sometimes I'll wait for five or six hours."

But the waiting and the jungle are not the worst part of his job for Butt. "The worst thing, the hardest thing, is just keeping from getting killed!" he says. There is an eight hundred dollar price tag on Butt's head; a bounty for anyone bringing in him or his rifle.

"I have to worry pretty much about snipers myself," Butt smiles. "And I worry a lot, because I know that man is aiming at me. When that lone sniper's bullet bounces off the rocks around you, you know you've been lucky! Maybe he just flinched, or the wind changed, or his target stumbled . . . if he missed he probably just had a bad break. Otherwise, he would have blown your head off!"

"That's how it is. You either make a mistake and miss, or you don't make a mistake and kill him. It's all in how good a shot you are and how good your technique is.

David's job is a brutal job. But there should be nothing surprising in that. And, at least Butt has the opportunity to be discriminating about whom he kills . . . in return he has to be able to withstand the pressure of the more personal nature of his killing. Looking at his rifle, or any soldier's rifle, brings back the crushingly true words of a Marine drill instructor to his new troops. "You're a hired killer, son. That's what you are, and that's what you're going to do! You're not a sign painter, or a car salesman, or a student or a teacher on anything nice . . . you're a hired killer!"

Night had crept in from the jungles and the men in Butt's tent had lit small red candles. Fresh milk had come down from battalion headquarters and Butt and the others were eagerly gulping huge quantities. They tilted back their heads and drank from foot and a half long aluminum illumination flare cannisters. The glow of the red candles, the reflections on the cannisters, the laughter and chatter of the Marines, and the racket of crickets lent an almost festive air to the tent. Outside, a group of ten Marines blacked their faces to go out on a night patrol across the river; soon they would be crouched in the bottom of the boat slipping across the silent water to begin their nightly agony.

In the tent one of Butt's friends called over;

"Hey. We got a patrol tomorrow?"

"Yep," another answered, "at three o'clock."

"Hey—that's right in the heat of the day!", the first man said unhappily.

"Naw—there's a breeze blowing in by then," commented a young Negro, from Texas.

"Well, where are we going?"

"North."

"You mean up to the other river?"

"Yeah."

"Across all those rice paddies?" The first Marine was sitting up now, apparently thoroughly concerned and dismayed.

"Yeah."

"HEY! There's a lot of gooks up there! Hey, Man!"

"Yeah."

"Oh, but they just aren't there between 1500 and 1900 right?", his tone was heavy with sarcasm.

"Yeah. RIGHT!". . . the whole tent grunted in unison.

The conversation turned to women . . . Vietcong women. The previous week a VC woman had jumped out of some bushes and wounded two Marines from this company. "Once a bitch up on the Hill was throwing grenades at us so fast she forgot to pull the pins on about half of them." Butt snorted at the thought and must have attemped a comparison beween these women and the coeds he had known at the University of Arkansas.

Butt took a big drink of milk. "I don't miss beer much; I never drank too much at home. But I sure do miss good cold water when I want it. I used to take water for granted, but never again.

The only other thing Butt misses is music. Armed Forces Radio plays some pretty good music, but it's hard to pick up where David works. And at home he's used to listening to his collection of classical records.

"The first thing I want to do when I get back is take a float trip," Butt smiled. "I know it sounds funny to want to get back into the woods again after having been over here for so long; but a float trip is so peaceful. I just want to go sit on that river and relax."

Suddenly the angry snap of bullets sounded in the night. The men in the tent rolled to the floor, rifles in hand. "Damn gooks!" growled Butt. "If they have to stay up at night for some reason, they'll throw a couple of rounds in here at us to make sure we stay up too!"

The men remained on the floor for some minutes. One man opened another box of combat rations . . . "Hey, anybody want some fruit cake?" he called. A chorus of no's greeted him.

"I can't see it . . . ." replied Butt. "If the rats at the Horseshoe won't eat the stuff, then I'm sure not going to eat it. I sure won't!"

After a while the men crawled off the floor and Butt spoke again. "These Vietnamese people are both intelligent and ignorant. They must have an extremely high resistance to disease. The way they live should kill anybody!"

"I'll tell you what make a Vietcong of one of these people," Butt said firmly. "A man goes out and hoes that hard rocky ground all day and tries to get a little crop growing. And then when he's just about to have a little success one of our big tanks come along and grinds his crop all to hell, and then we move a company of men through there. Hell! it wouldn't take but once for that to make me a Vietcong!" He gently moved his heavy sniper's rifle to a convenient position next to his cot. "But I'm a sniper on our team," he said and closed his eyes and went to sleep.

"It was an M-26 grenade that got us both," said the pale young Arkansas Marine from his hospital bed. "We were on a squad size patrol on Hill No. 270; the guy about twenty feet in front of me must have been the one who tripped it. Just all of a sudden there was this awful noise. It knocked me down. I was lying there . . . I never was unconscious . . . and I yelled for the corpsman right away. It's funny, I screamed for that corpsman immediately, maybe before I even hit the ground, but it seemed like I didn't yell for him until a long time later. I knew I was hit in the legs, but I could still move both my legs so I figured I was o.k. I didn't even know I was hit in the back until I got back to our base camp."

Lance Corporal Orus C. Pucket, Jr., 19, son of Mr. and Mrs. O. C. Puckett, Sr., of West Memphis, has been wounded four times in Vietnam. But, as is so often the case, most of the wounds were fairly small, so he wasn't evacuated, he received no purple hearts, and he was kept on duty. This time Orus got a purple heart.

One of the small consolations for Marines wounded in Vietnam, is the availability of the Hospital Ships, REPOSE and SANCTUARY. Both hospital ships, painted white with large red crosses on their sides and fully illuminated at all times, cruise the waters along the Vietnamese coast from the delta to the DMZ to care for the wounded. With a helicopter deck on its stern, the ship can receive wounded minutes after they have been hit. Once aboard, the wounded man has the benefit of a completely air-conditioned ship, with full medical staffs, and surgery facilities that provide everything from a frozen blood bank to an artificial heart machine. The REPOSE is listed as a non combatant ship according to the Geneva Conventions and is completely unarmed—even in enemy waters. There might be some question in the minds of the North Vietnamese as to the ships non-combatant status, however, since the ships presence allows the wounded to return to battle so much more quickly.

When Puckett was on board the REPOSE he was assigned to a large room with beds for about sixty patients. The room was used primarily for less serious injuries. Puckett was lying on a bottom bunk; the man above him called over to the Doctor: "Hey, Doc! How about getting this window cleaned off, so I can see lovely Vietnam?" The boy leaned back on the cool sheets and gloated over being here in this air conditioned room instead of out there. All the patients were dressed in light blue hospital gowns. A tape recorder on one bed blasted out a taped radio show someone had mailed from the states. The radio show was complete with month old newscasts.

"O.K., Puckett," said two young navy corpsmen. "Off to x-ray for you." Puckett looked as though he were used to the routine and managed to get onto the movable table with a minimum of distress. His heavily bandaged legs were clumsy and he looked a bit like he was taking a walk out of a space capsule as he swung onto the table. "Be right back," he said matter of factly.

As he moved down the hall, a conversation began between two of the other patients. "Hey, I saw that little blonde Red Cross girl today," said a skinny private from Missouri who had been wounded by a mortar. "She's not half as pretty as everybody said she was." He was obviously disappointed.

"Yeh, but she's got round eyes," his buddy retorted coolly. "She's American."

Most of the patients in the room had been wounded by shrapnel. One man, who was part of the ship's crew, had a ruptured appendix. Two other Marines had burns. "The burn cases increase during the rainy season," a nurse explained. The men start trying to figure a way to keep warm and dry and they usually pick the wrong way."

The room was less than half full of patients, and the nurse explained that was due to the fact that all the casualties that had been on board from the fire aboard the aircraft carrier, had been sent on back to the States.

Orus returned fully X-rayed. "I guess they'll be finding little pieces of steel in me for a long time," he mused. He nodded over to a cheerful young man limping through the door. "That guy has seventeen holes in him from neck to toes from shrapnel. They have him making two laps a day around the ship now to get walking right again."

The 1966 graduate of West Memphis High School settled

back onto the sheets. "I went straight from the high school to here," he explained. "A couple of buddies, Robert Wayne Thompson, and Garry Neal, and I decided to join up. We got out of high school in June—and I was here on December 29th, and on my way out on patrol as a machine gun team leader."

"You never know what's going to happen out there," Puckett said softly. We get most of our casualties from booby traps, and snipers. Snipers shot two of the guys in my platoon through the head on one operation. But, then, on Operation Union Two, I had a mortar round land about five feet in front of me . . . it was a dud. So, that's how it goes. Being away from home, in a strange country, knowing you might be killed . . . you can't think about all that. I really don't have time to think about it; they've always got me doing something."

Puckett has seen two other Marines from Arkansas since he got here: Jim Fowler of Ft. Smith and Johnny McCoy Thomas of DeValls Bluff. "Thomas got his orders to go home," smiled Puckett. "He's a heck of a guy." Thinking of home, Orus says he really misses American women—"the ones over here look like hell," he laughs.

While he was on R & R in the Philippines, he called his parents back in West Memphis. "I called them about two o'clock in the morning to make sure they'd be home. I just wanted to hear their voices. That really made me feel good. That, and getting mail from home. Mail is the best morale booster for everybody. If you didn't get mail, you'd go crazy."

Puckett was glad to be in the hospital. The rains had begun to fall and it was nice to be in an air conditioned room, with clean sheets, regular meals, and a roof over his head to keep out the rain. "The heat and cold I can take," he says. "But not the rain. When the rain starts I really get depressed." He looked around him. "Nobody bitches about being out here on the REPOSE."

Orus, isn't sure what he will do when he gets out of the Corps. "Could be one of a million things." A nurse brought the noon meal into the room. Orus brightened. "Boy that food is great!" His tray was piled with a minute steak, corn, rice, bread and butter, and apple pie. "I weighed 200 pounds when I came over here, and now I'm down to 185." He dug into the food— then slowed. "S' funny. I'm always hungry, but I can't seem to eat when the chow gets here . . . , it's great chow, the best I've had since I got in this country. Guess I'm just not used to having so much good food."

"I hope I get to sail with the ship to the Philippines before I go back ashore to duty," Puckett said and turned to look out the window. "It's been quite an experience to be here. Why am I here? Well, I'm just here . . . mainly because I got orders."

117